REMEMBERING

# CONSHOHOCKEN
## & west
# CONSHOHOCKEN

# REMEMBERING
# CONSHOHOCKEN
# & west
# CONSHOHOCKEN

## Jack Coll

Charleston · London

THE
History
PRESS

Published by The History Press
Charleston, SC 29403
www.historypress.net

All images are from the author's collection unless otherwise noted.

First published 2010

Manufactured in the United States

ISBN 978.1.59629.412.7

Library of Congress Cataloging-in-Publication Data

Coll, Jack.
Remembering Conshohocken and West Conshohocken / Jack Coll.
p. cm.
ISBN 978-1-59629-412-7
1. Conshohocken (Pa.)--History. 2. West Conshohocken (Pa.)--History. I. Title.
F159.C66C66 2010
974.8'12--dc22
2010025705

*Notice*: The information in this book is true and complete to the best of our knowledge. It is offered without guarantee on the part of the author or The History Press. The author and The History Press disclaim all liability in connection with the use of this book.

*I'd like to dedicate this book to Dave Pasquale, who didn't know much about Conshohocken and, like me, didn't do much reading. But Dave was my best friend who passed away, and certainly his community of friends miss him very much.*

# Contents

Acknowledgements     11

Introduction     13

**PART ONE. FROM INDIANS TO INDUSTRY**

Conshohocken Today     15

The Schuylkill River     16

The Leni-Lenape Indians     17

William Penn and the Trinket Purchase     19

Washington Takes the Stage, but Not in Conshohocken     20

It All Started with a Canal     21

The Birth of Industry in the Village     23

It's About Time to Incorporate     25

**PART TWO. CONSHOHOCKEN, THE FIRST HUNDRED YEARS**

Incorporation, It Really Started in Norristown     27

Let's Honor Edward "Ned" Hector     28

Early Leaders and Street Names     30

Everybody's Welcome, They Came Looking for America     32

The Bridge—Matson's Ford, That Is     37

# CONTENTS

**PART THREE. INDUSTRY**

It All Started with a Shovel Head                                43

John Elwood Lee, What a Man                                      45

Newton and Hervey, the Walker Brothers                          48

The Quaker Chemical Story                                        50

Alan C. Hale, Almost a Century                                  52

And There's More                                                53


**PART FOUR. THE UNIFORMS: POLICE, FIREMEN AND MILITARY**

Police                                                          57

Washington Fire Company                                         70

New Century, New Fire Company                                   77

Conshohocken Military                                           80


**PART FIVE. A LITTLE EDUCATION ON SCHOOLS**

It Started Immediately                                          85

Montgomery County Taps the Best                                 87

Catholics, Conshohocken Was the First                           88

Say Goodbye to the Public School                                89

Conshohocken Community College                                  90


**PART SIX. SPORTS**

Baseball, the Fact and the Funny                                93

Football, Tough as Steel                                        97

Basketball, It's About the Hall of Fame                         99

And All the Rest                                                101


**PART SEVEN. BUSINESS**

It Started Slow                                                 107

Fayette Street Was a Boom                                       109

Family Businesses Still Doing Business                          112

# CONTENTS

**PART EIGHT. A FEW CONSHOHOCKEN GEMS**

Hannibal Hamlin, a Guest of the Woods     115

Governor John F. Kennedy Misses Conshohocken     115

The First Lady, During and After     117

Finally, Conshohocken Gets a Presidential Visit     117

The Pines     118

Conshohocken's Only Hospital     120

Bishop Matthew Simpson, the President and Conshohocken     121

That's Right, Owner of the Philadelphia Phillies     122

Just a Few More Names     123


About the Author     127

# Acknowledgements

In order to tell all these stories accurately, I would like to acknowledge the following sources: *The History of Montgomery County*, by William J. Buck; Historical Society of Montgomery County, which can be contacted at (610) 272-0297 or www.hsmcpa.org; *History of Montgomery County*, vols. 1 and 2, 1884, by Theodore W. Bean; *History of Montgomery County*, vol. 1, 1923, by Clifton S. Hunsicker; *History of Montgomery County*, vols. 1 and 2, 1983, edited by Jean Barth Toll and Michael J. Schwager; Lenni Lenape Historical Society, Allentown, Pennsylvania; Bryon Anderson at the Abraham Lincoln Presidential Library and Museum; *Neighborhood Tales*, by Samuel Gordon Smyth; *Norristown Times Herald*; *Conshohocken Recorder*; the Conshohocken Free Library, 301 Fayette Street, Conshohocken, (610) 825-1656; Lower Merion Historical Society, Gerald A Francis, president; Bob Brodie, Main Street Photo, Dave Wingeron, manager; *Walker of Conshohocken*, by H. Alan Dunn; *History of the Alan Wood Iron and Steel Company*, prepared by Frank H. Taylor; J. Ellwood Lee Company, Conshohocken, Pennsylvania, 1883–1908, Silver Anniversary; Gene Walsh for his quick and excellent work on the cover photograph.

A special thanks to all the residents who have contributed to this book in one way or another over the years. A few of the good storytellers I've had the pleasure to know over the years include John "Chick" McCarter, Art "Tuti" Andrey, Sam Januzelli, John Durante, Paul "Roger" Touhey, George Snear, Rudy Lincul, Bill Danitz, Dr. Joseph Leary, Vilma Frattone and Gerald McTamney.

Thanks to my wife, Donna, who proofreads every single thing that I write, and for the support of my loving children, Brian and Jackie.

# Introduction

The history of Conshohocken, Pennsylvania, is made up of more than 160 years of small stories. Sometimes those stories are centered on the Schuylkill River or in one of the long-forgotten mills. These stories come from the living rooms of the immigrants who came to Conshohocken looking for the American dream, and they come from the firemen and other volunteers who protect and serve this great community.

When you read some of these stories, you'll wonder why this book wasn't titled *Conshohocken: I Didn't Know That*, because that's what you'll be saying time and time again. *Remembering Conshohocken and West Conshohocken* serves not so much as a recorded history of this borough as it takes the reader back in time, but rather as a reminder of the foundation of this borough: the residents. No matter how far back we go in time, this borough is and always will be about our residents, the changes they made and the contributions we all continue to make.

Conshohocken celebrates Veteran's Day, Memorial Day and Independence Day, all with good reason: our involvement in the struggle for freedom goes back to the Revolutionary War, the Civil War and all the wars since. Our involvement in sports goes back nearly 125 years; our involvement in firefighting goes back more than 135 years; and our ancestors arrived in Conshohocken more than 175 years ago.

In 1905, Father Benedict Tomiak of St. Mary's Church founded the St. Mary's Orphanage for Polish Boys. The orphanage consisted of about a dozen orphans from the city of Philadelphia. Father Benedict Tomiak purchased the former George Bullock estate in West Conshohocken and opened the St. Mary's Orphans Asylum for both boys and girls. In 1936, the Sisters of the Holy Nazareth purchased a castle in Ambler once owned by Richard Vanselous Mattison, and St. Mary's Orphanage moved to Ambler and was later renamed St. Mary's Villa for Children.

In 1965, Hollywood visited St. Mary's Villa in Ambler to use the orphanage as a backdrop for a movie. The movie script was based on the memoir written by Jane Trahey called *Mother Superior*, the original title for the film, later changed to *The Trouble with Angels*. The movie starred Rosalind Russell and Hayley Mills. Russell played Mother Superior, while Mills played Mary Clancy, who was sent to an all girls' Catholic boarding school. To think that it all started in Conshohocken.

Hey, I didn't know that. Read on.

# Part One

# From Indians to Industry

## CONSHOHOCKEN TODAY

Conshohocken, Pennsylvania, is a one-square-mile community located thirteen miles northwest of Philadelphia and five miles east of Valley Forge National Park. It is a thriving community of nine thousand residents, ten churches with thirteen different denominations and a history dating back to William Penn.

A stroll down Fayette Street, Conshohocken's main street named after General Lafayette, gives visitors and residents a great sense of history and twenty-first-century progression. The former mansions of John Elwood Lee—currently Conshohocken's Borough Hall—and the former Jones Estate—currently the Ciavarelli Funeral Home—are to this day simply breathtaking.

The Great American Pub and Flanigan's Boathouse restaurants stand out in the business district, along with Light Parker Furniture, Flocco's Discount Shoes and Reliance Federal Credit Union. Places to eat are plentiful, including Fayette Street Grille, Spampinato's Restaurant, Ted's Pizza, Win Wah Inn, Chiangmai and Tony and Joe's Pizzeria. A few restaurants off the beaten path include Pasta Via Italian restaurant and Stone Rose, located on upper Fayette Street, and Vince Totaro's Trattoria Restaurant, located on Spring Mill Avenue. The borough also offers many specialty stores and shops, like Conshohocken Italian Bakery, founded in 1973 by Domenico Gambone and Frank Manze.

Conshohocken is the quintessential all-American, main-street town, with an extraordinary history setting it apart from any other small town in America.

The borough of Conshohocken seen along the banks of the Schuylkill River, where the Lenape Indians once thrived, before being displaced by the Industrial Revolution. *Photo by Brian Coll.*

# THE SCHUYLKILL RIVER

Conshohocken is a town built on a hill overlooking the Schuylkill River, pronounced Sku-kel, or Skoo-kull. The river is approximately 130 miles long and lies entirely within the state of Pennsylvania. The first known name of the river was Ganshohawanee, meaning "rushing and roaring waters," presumably for the falls at the fault line near what is now the Fairmount Water Works. The name was given by the Delaware Indians, who were thought to be the original settlers of the area along the banks of the river.

There seems to be somewhat of a dispute as to who named the river the Schuylkill; after all, the Leni-Lenape Indians are considered some of the original inhabitants of the area. The Leni-Lenape migrated to the valley from the Mississippi Valley, taking advantage of the climate, river and rich planting grounds. It was the Indians who named the river the Schuylkill, meaning Hidden River. But a European discoverer named Arendt Corssen was one of the first Westerners to explore the area and

This photograph of the Spring Mill Ferry and Inn is perhaps the oldest photograph of the Conshohocken area. The ferry was established in the late 1700s, and the inn was owned and operated by Reese Harry from 1804 until his death in 1824. The inn was located on the west side of the Schuylkill in the Spring Mill section of the borough.

sailed right past the mouth of the river. Corssen, who explored for the Dutch East Indies Company, was said to have named the river "Schuyl-Kil" because of the reeds, sedges and high grasses that hid the mouth of the river.

## THE LENI-LENAPE INDIANS

In the early 1500s, a group of Indians calling themselves the Leni-Lenape settled in an unspoiled wilderness in what is known today as northern Delaware, New Jersey, parts of New York and eastern Pennsylvania, including what is Conshohocken.

The Leni-Lenape Indian tribe settled on Edge Hill (Conshohocken) and called their home *Gueno Sheiki-Hacki-Ing* or *Gueneuschigihacking—Gueneu* meaning

This portrait of Tish-Co-Han, an early Lenape chief, was painted by Hesselius, a Swedish artist. Tish-Co-Han means "he who never blackens himself." In 1737, Tish-Co-Han signed the treaty known as the Walking Purchase. He was considered by members of the William Penn family as an honest, upright Indian. *Courtesy of Lower Merion Historical Society.*

"long," *schigi* meaning "fine," *hacki* meaning "land," with the locative *ing*, having the significance "at the long fine land." The name Leni-Lenape is redundant, as if to say "the common ordinary people." Lenape by itself is sufficient. The Lenape were composed of three different groups with a couple minor differences.

The Lenape Indians were family oriented and did not seek hostile confrontations. They would always locate their villages near streams or rivers, where fishing for food and easy transportation made for easier living. The Lenape always fertilized the land with the planting of corn, beans, pumpkins, squash and tobacco. They lived in permanent villages and would only leave in their quest for food, furs and trade. The Indians did not live in teepees but rather in wigwams or longhouses that were much more permanent structures.

William Penn, who was credited with the planning and development of the city of Philadelphia, developed very good relations with the Lenape Indians. By 1683, after more than 150 years of the Lenape living along the river, Penn signed a treaty that would eventually lead to the demise of the tribe in Pennsylvania. Over the next two centuries, the Lenape Indians were moved to smaller territories, and by the 1860s, most of the Lenape remaining in the eastern United States had been sent to the Oklahoma Territory. Today, what's left of the Lenape nation lives in several parts of the United States, including Oklahoma, Wisconsin and Kansas.

## WILLIAM PENN AND THE TRINKET PURCHASE

William Penn, founder of the state of Pennsylvania, was a devout Quaker and very well respected by the Lenape Indians. He gained the trust of the Indians after signing several treaties, including the treaty that secured the village of Conshohocken.

Penn purchased Conshohocken, or at the time *Gueno Sheiki-Hacki-Ing*, as part of a much larger land deal with the Indians. In William Penn's deed of 1683, the lands between the Schuylkill and Chester Rivers, the line of the purchase, commenced "on the West side of Manaiunk [Schuylkill River] called Conshohocken." (The river is now spelled Manayunk, meaning "where we go to drink.") The deed was penned by Secane and Icquoquehan. It also stated as part of the agreement that the lands east of the Schuylkill to Pemmapecka Creek run "So Farr as ye hill called Conshockin on the said river Manaiunk." The deed was signed by Neneshickan, Malebore and Neshanocke.

A couple of years later, in 1685, Penn again agreed with the Indians for more land "Beginning at the hill called Conshohockin on the River Manaiunck of Skoolkill." This deed was signed by Shakahoppoh, Secane, Malibor and Tangoras.

Ownership pertaining to much of the deeded land would later be questioned due to the price Penn paid. Legend has it that Penn traded flashy trinkets for the land. The Indians believed that Penn was merely renting and sharing the land. The Lenape couldn't understand how any one person could own land. They lived in a world where the air they breathed was free, the wilderness around them, the river, the animals and the land were for everyone to share, not own. All the while, Penn had Indians sign legal deeds to the land, but the Indians never owned the land in the first place and legally were in no position to sell it.

## Washington Takes the Stage, but Not in Conshohocken

The American Revolutionary War began as a war between the kingdom of Great Britain and thirteen united former British colonies in North America and concluded as a global war between several European great powers. The war that began in 1775 and was fought in several locations, including the eastern seaboard and northwest territories, came to Conshohocken on December 11, 1777.

General George Washington and the Continental army successfully held off British attacks in the Battle of Whitemarsh (December 5–8, 1777). On the morning of December 11, Washington's troops marched through Conshohocken, crossed the river at Matson's Ford and set up camp in Gulph Mills. General John Sullivan ordered wagons tied together to form a bridge at Matson's Ford so his troops could cross the river. Once on the

General Gilbert du Motier, Marquis de Lafayette, was at the center of a skirmish that took place during the Revolutionary War at the foot of the Matson's Ford Bridge in Conshohocken. On May 20, 1778, Lafayette used the little-known Barren Hill path to escape General William Howe of the British command. Lafayette's men encountered a fight that turned bloody when eight Americans and four Indian scouts were killed.

West Conshohocken side of the river, Sullivan met with resistance from two thousand British troops led by Lord Cornwallis. Sullivan ordered his troops to retreat back across the makeshift bridge, destroying the bridge as they retreated. Sullivan led his troops to Swedesford crossing in Norristown and arrived in Gulph Mills on December 13 in a heavy snowstorm. Six days later, the order was given to march seven miles on West Gulph Road to Valley Forge to meet with Washington and endure one of the coldest winters in history.

On May 20, 1778, the Revolutionary War once again was a focal point in Conshohocken, where the results were deadly. The skirmish centered on a twenty-year-old general named Gilbert du Motier, Marquis de Lafayette. General Lafayette was General George Washington's favorite and most loyal foreign officer. The young Frenchman departed from Valley Forge on May 18, 1778, with more than 2,200 Continental soldiers, heading toward Philadelphia. Lafayette's troops camped at Barren Hill, ten miles outside Valley Forge.

On May 20, General Lafayette was surprised to learn that his troops were surrounded by five of the most experienced generals, ready to attack. Lafayette met with his men outside St. Peter's Lutheran Church and decided that two generals, Enoch Poor and James Varnem, would lead the troops down a hidden path and into Conshohocken.

That hidden path was later named Barren Hill Road. The road led Lafayette and his troops to the Matson's Ford crossing. The troops crossed into the hills of what later would be West Conshohocken, but not without a skirmish. An attack at the foot of the Matson's Ford crossing on the Conshohocken side of the river, currently Fayette Street, left eight Americans and four Indian scouts dead from British gunfire. All twelve of the dead were buried at St. Peter's cemetery in Barren Hill.

General George Washington was very impressed with Lafayette's great escape. Conshohocken's Fayette Street was named after the general, as was Lafayette Hill in nearby Whitemarsh Township. Conshohocken also named a street after General George Washington, but despite all the speculation over the past two hundred years, George Washington never stepped foot inside Conshohocken's boundaries.

## It All Started with a Canal

In the early 1800s, the Schuylkill River was used primarily as a means of transportation for moving goods, particularly coal. However, as the demand for coal grew from the increased mills along the lower end of the

The canal system along the Schuylkill River was constructed over a twelve-year period, from 1816 to 1828, and covered 108 miles, including Conshohocken. This Conshohocken Canal photograph shows a barge dredging the canal in the 1920s, allowing heavier shipments of goods to travel to Philadelphia.

river, the shallow Schuylkill River became tougher to navigate with heavier loads of coal.

Josiah White and Erskine Hazard owned and operated a rolling mill that produced nails and wire at the falls of the Schuylkill (East Falls). The partners depended on coal shipments from the coal region located in upstate Pennsylvania and needed a cost-effective method of shipping the product. In 1815, White and Hazard organized the Schuylkill Navigation Company and petitioned the State of Pennsylvania for the right to make the river navigable.

Work began on the Schuylkill Canal system in 1816 with the building of a dam at the falls of the Schuylkill, followed by Flat Rock Dam. In just twelve years, the company constructed 108 miles of the canal system, starting at the Fairmount Dam in Philadelphia to just below Pottstown. With 46 miles of slack water, or pools created by dams, the 62 miles of actual canals included 120 locks, including one in the Connaughtown section of Conshohocken.

The canal was completed in Conshohocken in 1824 and was a shot in the arm to local industry. Mules would pull the boats loaded with cargo along the canal in and out of the city of Philadelphia. In 1831, John Wood and his son Alan walked along the towpath of this canal looking for a location for their iron mill. Once inside the Conshohocken village boundaries, the father and son team decided that the canal could not only provide the rolling mill with transportation but also with power, with a water wheel.

The Woods entered into an agreement with the Schuylkill Navigation Company for the use of the land and water, signing a yearly lease of twenty-five cents per running foot of land and an annual rent of $1,000, giving them the right to use the canal's water. Following the completion of the canal, the company sold a majority of the land to James Wells, who later opened the Ford Hotel and Railroad Depot. Cadwallader Foulke also purchased a large tract of land from the canal company and established a large farm in lower Conshohocken. Foulk agreed to a deal with the canal company to use water from the canal for his crops. Other property on the west side was later sold to members of the Wood, Tracey, O'Brien, Hallowell, Trewendt and Jones families as well.

In 1949, the Schuylkill Navigation Company declared bankruptcy and deeded all its properties to the Commonwealth of Pennsylvania. The canal was in operation as late as 1925, but only a handful of boats remained in operation. Today, what remains of the canal system is mainly used for recreational purposes. A great view of the canal still exists in the Manayunk section of Philadelphia just behind Main Street.

## The Birth of Industry in the Village

The only businesses that thrived in the small Conshohocken village were basically those that catered to the travelers who used the river to move goods and weary horse and carriage travelers. By the 1830s, the David Harry Gristmill had long been established, as was Simons Clothing Store. Richard Thomas owned and operated an old mill, and the Seven Stars Hotel just outside of town had been established since the early 1700s.

But the majority of the businesses were blacksmith shops, including John Wagner's blacksmith shop on the west side of the river, with two black- and whitesmith shops in the village (a whitesmith shop makes silver kitchen utensils).

The businesses that really thrived were the taverns and inns along the Schuylkill, like the Spring Mill Inn and Ferry owned and operated for a time by Reese Harry. Peter Legaux had established Spring Mill Inn and Ferry years earlier under an act of assembly in 1789. Flatboats were used to carry loads of ox teams across the river in a safe manner. The main rope stretched across the river, with guide ropes on both sides of the cable. The occupants of the boats could propel themselves back and forth across the river.

Conshohocken industry was the family foundation for more than a century in the borough, with Alan Wood Steel leading the dozens of steel and other mills that called Conshohocken home. This photograph shows Frank Staley on the left with his co-worker at the Schuylkill Ironworks in 1907.

While a few small businesses flourished in the Conshohocken village, it was the canal that led to the formation of J. Wood & Son Iron Company. On September 3, 1831, James Wood and his son Alan entered into agreement with the Schuylkill Navigation Company. The Woods would rent, and later purchase, the ground along the canal. The land was described as being on Matson's Ford road between the canal and Schuylkill River fronting Mill Street. The Wood family and the Wood business would play a large part in the incorporation of the borough. The Wood family would enjoy more than a century of success in Conshohocken.

# It's About Time to Incorporate

By the mid-1840s, the village of Conshohocken was a thriving community. Washington Street, named after General George Washington, was originally laid out as the main corridor in the village. Washington Street made sense, as it ran parallel to the Schuylkill River and canal. Industries and some retail outlets set up along the river and canal path.

But with the completion of the Schuylkill Canal in 1824 and the addition of small industry, the village grew in leaps and bounds. The Philadelphia, Germantown and Norristown Railroad was built in 1835 and quickly played a prominent role in the village for both transportation and the shipping of goods.

The Conshohocken Post Office was established in 1836 and was located in the Ford Hotel and Train Depot.

In 1833, Conshohocken had one store, one tavern, a rolling mill, a gristmill and six dwellings. A census from the 1830s identifies the homeowners as David Harry, Cadwallader Foulke, Isaac Jones, Dan Freedley and C. Jacoby. While not mentioned by name, it is believed that Edward Hector was the sixth homeowner in the village. Conshohocken also had its first bridge over the Schuylkill River, a covered bridge owned and operated as a toll bridge by the Matsonford Bridge Company.

In the 1840s, the job market grew with the addition of Stephen Colwell opening up his blast furnace in both Conshohocken and Plymouth Township. Colwell's lime was a product needed by the Wood Company. Colwell's limestone quarries in Plymouth Township and James Wood & Son Iron Mill increased the job market. With the additional jobs came the workers and their families.

With the addition of residents came retail. The well-traveled paths running through the village quickly became roads—dirt roads, of course. Coupled with the increased river and canal traffic, along with the railroad, transient workers followed. Retail businesses like John Pugh's Flour, Feed and Grocery Store, blacksmith shops, clothing stores, hardware stores and a few service shops pushed up the hill to Fayette Street.

It wasn't long before lawlessness followed. No one was responsible for repairing the washed-out dirt roads following a hard rain. With no rules or laws to govern the people, it became clear that it was time to incorporate.

Part Two

# Conshohocken,
# the First Hundred Years

## INCORPORATION, IT REALLY STARTED IN NORRISTOWN

The first incarnation of the United States Post Office was established by Benjamin Franklin in Philadelphia in 1775 by a decree of the Second Continental Congress. The Conshohocken Post Office was one of the early offices established in 1836, outside city limits. It was located in the Ford Hotel and Train Depot located on the east side of the new covered bridge, alongside the train tracks and canal. In the early 1830s, the hotel and train depot were the hub of activity in the village.

By the mid-1840s, industry was growing. The increased industry brought jobs into the village, and with the jobs came families. That led to needed retail and service stores. During this decade, members of the busy Conshohocken village started talking about incorporation, recognizing the need for a governing body in the town.

In 1848, five members of the village were selected to apply for a charter of incorporation and select a name for the town. James Wood, James Wells, Isaac Jones, David Harry and Cadwallader Foulke were selected to complete the incorporation proceedings.

The five members of the committee were a diverse group. James Wood, owner and manager of the J. Wood & Sons Company, was selected chairman of the committee. James Wells was the proprietor of the Ford Hotel and Railroad Depot and for a time served as Montgomery County sheriff. Isaac Jones was president of the Matsonford Bridge Company, a privately owned toll bridge, until 1886, when Montgomery County purchased the bridge.

David Harry was a gristmill owner and operator who also owned a large chunk of property in the village, and Cadwallader Foulke was a farmer in Plymouth Township on the border of the Schuylkill River whose land reached into the Connaughtown section of Conshohocken.

The 5 members of the incorporation committee represented the 727 residents of the village. With the residents' approval, the 5 men met in Norristown at the Montgomery Hotel in 1848 and decided on three possible names for the borough. They agreed to write the three names on separate slips of paper and drop them into Isaac Jones's beaver hat. According to the writings of Samuel Gordon Smyth (1859–1930), an early author for the Montgomery and Bucks County Historical Societies, it was James Wells who scribbled out "Conshohocken" on a slip of paper and dropped it into the hat. The other two names submitted were "Riverside" and "Wooddale." The committee agreed that the third name drawn from the hat would be the name used for incorporation. Smyth reported that James Wells had the honor of drawing the three names, the third being "Conshohocken."

On May 15, 1850, Conshohocken became the third borough in Montgomery County, following Norristown, established in 1812, and Pottstown, 1815. Pennsylvania's governor, William Fraeme Johnson, signed the document of incorporation, and on May 18, 1850, the incorporation papers were delivered by train on the Philadelphia, Norristown & Germantown line.

Several hundred residents (nearly the whole town) waited anxiously at the Conshohocken depot on May 18, when the train pulled into the station on time and the conductor of the train handed the sack of mail to the Conshohocken postmaster, who reached in and pulled out the official papers of incorporation. In turn, the postmaster handed the incorporation papers to Conshohocken's first burgess (mayor), John Wood, son of ironmaster James Wood, who officially announced to the cheering residents that they now lived in the borough of Conshohocken.

## LET'S HONOR EDWARD "NED" HECTOR

Edward "Ned" Hector came to settle in Conshohocken in 1827, long after his honorable discharge from the American Revolutionary army. Hector was one of Conshohocken's early settlers and the first known African American resident of this borough. Hector settled into a log cabin that at that time was on the outskirts of the village, located on the corner of what was to become Harry Street and Barren Hill Road, a block off the main path (Fayette Street).

Edward Hector was a private in Captain Hercules Courtney's company of Pennsylvania Artillery, mustered on March 10, 1777, by Lord Sprogell, a commissary general of musters.

In September 1777, Private Hector, in the military just six months, faced a life or death situation at the Battle of Brandywine. At that battle in Chester County, Captain Courtney's troops came under heavy fire, and many casualties were suffered, including one of Hector's contemporaries, John Francis. Francis, a fellow African American Patriot from Pennsylvania, lost both his legs at the Battle of Brandywine. Francis served under Captain Eppel and Colonel Craig and was pensioned out of service less than a year later.

Under heavy fire and many casualties, all troops were ordered to abandon their posts and retreat in an effort to save lives. Private Hector, an ammunition wagon driver, disobeyed the order to retreat and alone worked his way back onto the battlefield. Under heavy enemy fire, Hector recovered his team of horses and hitched the ammunition wagon, stopping to gather weapons left behind by the soldiers who had fallen victim to enemy fire.

Hector's heroics saved the day for the American forces and allowed the troops to recover and prevent the British from benefiting from the ammo wagons and supplies. Hector's heroism was noted in the history of the Revolutionary War records and can be found in the Pennsylvania Archives.

Edward "Ned" Hector passed away in January 1834, and his obituary, found in the *Norristown Register* from January 15, 1834, read in part:

*Edward Hector, a colored man and veteran of the Revolution. Obscurity in life and oblivion is too often the lot of the worthy, they pass away and no "storied Stone" perpetuates the remembrance of their noble actions. The humble subject of this notice will doubtless share the common fate. He has joined the great assembly of the dead and will soon be forgotten, and yet, many a monument had been "reared to some proud son of earth" who less deserved it than poor old Ned. His earlier and better days were devoted to the cause of the American Revolution; in that cause he risked all he had to risk his life and he survived the event for a long lapse of years to witness the prosperity of a country whose independence he had so nobly assisted to achieve, and which neglected him in his old age.*

Hector's obituary in the *Norristown Register* was really quite an honor in that newspapers at that time didn't post obituaries for members of the African American community.

Hector was buried in Upper Merion Township. His wife, Jude, died on the way home from the burial. Hector had applied to Congress three times for his pension over the years after the war, and at the age of eighty-nine, a year before he died, he received a token payment of forty dollars.

In 1853, three years after the borough of Conshohocken incorporated and nineteen years after Hector's death, borough council, led by Burgess John Wood, passed a measure to rename Barren Hill Road from Fayette Street to North Lane in honor of Edward "Ned" Hector. Many of the councilmen in 1853 had known Ned personally and felt honored to rename Barren Hill Road "Hector Street."

A historical marker furnished by the Pennsylvania Museum and Historical Commission was dedicated on September 19, 1976, honoring Hector. The marker sits at the northeast corner of what are now West Hector and Fayette Streets. The marker is located less than one hundred yards from the site of Hector's cabin, later demolished to make way for St. Matthew's first church.

The iron marker reads: "Private in Captain Hercules Courtney's Company, Third Pa. Artillery Continental Line, in the Battle of Brandywine. His home was in Conshohocken. He is symbolic of the many unknown Black soldiers who served in the American Revolution, but whose race is not mentioned in muster rolls."

## EARLY LEADERS AND STREET NAMES

Conshohocken's streets were named after prominent early settlers of the borough. The five men involved in the incorporation proceedings all had streets named after them or their families. James Wood, ironmaster, known as the "Father of Conshohocken," and his son James, who was the borough's first burgess and later elected a United States congressman, were honored with the naming of **Wood Street**.

David Harry, who purchased 1,250 acres of ground from Jasper Farmer in 1700, was remembered on the entire east side of the borough. Harry's grandson, also named David, was involved in the incorporation, and for many years the Harry family served in prominent positions in the borough, hence the name **Harry Street**.

David Jones purchased 160 acres from the Harry family in 1754. Isaac Jones, a descendant of David, was a farmer and businessman and the borough's third incorporator. Isaac was also the president of the Matsonford Bridge Company for many years. The Jones family had very deep roots in the village and later the borough, so it made sense that the borough would have a **Jones Street**.

**Wells Street** was named after James Wells, who also was a signer of the incorporation papers. Wells owned and operated the Ford Hotel and Train Depot located alongside the river and canal. The fifth signer of incorporation was Cadwallader Foulke, a member of the Plymouth Meeting Friends Society. Foulke owned and operated a farm in the Connaughtown section of the borough, where **Foulke Street** was located.

William Hallowell was a member of the borough's first council in 1850 and later served as the borough's burgess in 1856 and again from 1862 to 1864. Hallowell built his handsome Victorian home on the corner of West Seventh Avenue and Forest Street; the building still stands today as an apartment house, but for some odd reason **Hallowell Street** is located on the east side of the borough. Hallowell was in the construction business and built Conshohocken's Baptist Presbyterian Church and the Patriotic Order Sons of America Building located at Second Avenue and Fayette Street (the current location of Tony & Joe's Pizzeria), among other prominent buildings of the day.

John Righter married Elizabeth Legaux, a descendant of Peter Legaux. Righter owned a good portion of the Legaux property located in the Spring Mill section of the borough and, in 1909, sold twenty-three acres to John Elwood Lee. **Righter Street** runs behind what would become Lee Tire and Rubber Company of Conshohocken.

Stephen Colwell had his iron and lime business throughout the Conshohocken and Plymouth area and conducted a portion of his business with the J. Wood & Sons Company. Colwell would smelt his iron into ingots and transport them along a dirt path that he cut through the woods on the lower west side of the borough. Because of the location of the trail, often Colwell's horses and wagons were the only travelers to be found on the trail, a trail that became known as Colwell's Lane. The name never changed, and even when the more modern highways pushed through the name remained **Colwell Lane**. It wasn't until 1966, under the pressure of the Conshohocken Chamber of Commerce led by George Gunning, that the borough opened up the lower half of Colwell Lane to traffic.

Members of the Forrest family were early business leaders in the borough and built two large buildings on Marble Street and what later would become

**Forrest Street**. One of the buildings was the Forrest Hotel. Members of the family were sensitive to the borough's needs and often supported them in times of need.

John Freedley had limekilns located along the banks of the Plymouth Creek between Ridge and Germantown Pike. Dr. Freedley lived in an area known as Ivory Rock, and his house was later used by the Alan Wood Steel Company as offices. The name **Freedley Street** appears on area maps dating back to 1848, two years before the borough's incorporation.

**Sutcliffe Lane** sits at the base of Sutcliffe Park, developed in the early 1960s. Sutcliffe Lane sits on a former dairy farm. In 1929, Frank Sutcliffe was president of the former John Wood Manufacturing Company and president of a realty firm that developed most of the upper portion of the borough. Sutcliffe donated thirty-nine acres of land to be used as a park in honor of his wife, Mary Jane.

As a side note, street names on the lower east side named after trees, like **Walnut**, **Cherry**, **Poplar**, **Elm**, **Ash** and **Apple** Streets, came as a result of David Harry's nursery once being located throughout the lower half of the borough. The streets were properly named after the trees once grown on the site.

**Spring Mill Avenue** was named because it was the road that led to Bubbling Springs, once located in the Spring Mill section of the borough.

As stated earlier, **Hector Street** was named after Edward "Ned" Hector, **Washington Street was** named after General George Washington and **Fayette Street** was named after General Gilbert du Motier, Marquis de Lafayette.

## EVERYBODY'S WELCOME, THEY CAME LOOKING FOR AMERICA

When the borough incorporated in 1850, Conshohocken had 727 residents. By 1860, the population had grown to 1,741 residents. In 1870, the population had jumped to 3,071, and nearly six hundred houses dotted the landscape. Although there were only three farms within the borough limits, there were twenty-eight different places of industry, and industry equaled immigrant opportunity.

In the 1820s, many Irish settlers found work with the Schuylkill Navigation Company, which began work in 1816 on a 108-mile stretch of canal beginning in Port Carbon and running through five counties, including the

Members of the Cianelli family gathered on the front porch of their West Second Avenue Home in 1923 for this group photograph. Teresa Cianelli is seated on the steps, second from left in the front row. Teresa's mother, Clara, is seated in the center of the row dressed in black, and Dominick is on the far right, standing. It wasn't uncommon for immigrants to come to this country and live with relatives until they found jobs in the mills. *Courtesy of Theresa Manley.*

borough of Conshohocken. Many of these Irish immigrants settled in the Norristown area. By the mid-1830s, the Irish had begun construction of St. Patrick's Catholic Church in Norristown, the first Catholic church in Montgomery County.

In 1841 and again in 1847, thousands of Irish immigrants poured into Montgomery County to escape from the destitution in Ireland when droughts ruined the potato fields, leading to family evictions. The need to survive sent them to America. From 1820 to 1850, more than four million Irish fled their native land to look for the American dream, and many of them found it in Conshohocken. By 1880, 78 percent of Conshohocken's population was foreign-born, and these immigrants found jobs as laborers and later owned land in Conshohocken.

According to the 1870 census, approximately 25 percent of Conshohocken's 3,071 residents were born in Ireland. Many Irish found work building the first railroads along the Schuylkill River and working in the many Conshohocken

Ilde Manetti poses with her five children in 1934 in the "Field of Daises," once located at the far end of West Third Avenue behind the bocce club, seen in the background. Ilda's five children are Gloria and Vilma in the front row and Ruth, Louis and Marie in the back row. *Courtesy of Vilma Manetti Frattone.*

mills. By 1856, the Conshohocken Irish had built St. Matthew's Roman Catholic Church at the corner of Hector and Harry Streets.

By 1900, Irish residents made up most of the town's population, many of them opening businesses along the ninety-foot-wide dirt road called Fayette Street. In 2009, residents of Irish descent made up more than 25 percent of Conshohocken's population, making it the largest ethnic group of residents in the borough.

From 1880 to 1900, immigrants began arriving from Poland looking for the same work that would allow them to become landowners, as the Irish had before them. According to the 1880 census, a number of Polish immigrants arrived and lived along the Schuylkill River in Upper Merion Township, including Swedeland. With jobs available in the many stone quarries and woolen mills, the Polish immigrants expanded into Bridgeport and Conshohocken, where women and children also found jobs.

By 1905, Conshohocken was the first town in Montgomery County to support a Catholic church strictly for Polish immigrants. St. Mary's Church

In 1938, a group of West Third Avenue residents gathered for a block photograph. From left to right, the four ladies standing in the back include Jeannie Cardamone, Frankina Agustinelli, Lucky Androni and Mrs Androni. In the front row from left were Angie Santoni, Mrs. Santoni, Marie Manetti and her mother, Ilda Manetti. The back of West Fourth Avenue can be seen in the background; notice the outhouse on the right. Outhouses were very commonplace into the 1950s in Conshohocken. *Courtesy of Vilma Manetti Frattone.*

was founded in 1905, followed by Sacred Heart Church in Swedesburg, founded in 1906. The founding of St. Mary's Church led to many Polish-owned business in the area of West Elm and Maple Streets. By 1980, one-third of the borough's residents were of Polish descent. According to the latest census, Polish residents currently make up 13 percent of the borough's population.

Opportunities for skilled and unskilled labor continued along the Schuylkill corridor due to all the textile mills in Norristown. Bridgeport offered many opportunities in the carpet and woolen mills, and opportunities abounded in the steel mills of Conshohocken.

Italian immigrants started drifting into Montgomery County about 1850. But it wasn't until the 1880s that a growing population in their own country made it difficult to find work, leading to economic hardships particularly in southern Italy and Sicily. Italians began arriving in Conshohocken about 1900 and took jobs in the nearby quarries, steel mills and on the railroad, and by 1909, they found work on the Pennsylvania Western (P&W) Rail line. Hundreds of Italians were employed for several years while the lines were under construction. Ten years later, in 1919, many Italians found work for Montgomery County building the new concrete Matsonford Bridge. Many of the families gathered from the old country and began opening up businesses in the lower part of town along Maple Street from Elm to Fifth Avenue. That section of Conshohocken—formerly known as "Cork Row" because of the heavy Irish population—became known as "Little Italy." According to the 1970 census, more than 30 percent of the borough's population at that time was Italian.

Germans had been working the Pennsylvania farms long before 1800, but when the Industrial Revolution swept through Montgomery County from 1870 to 1910, German immigrants from the western part of their country migrated to this country with industrial skills and dreams of purchasing land. Conshohocken became home to many German immigrants who, like other immigrants, found work in the glass factories, steel mills, woolen mills and Lee's Surgical Supply Factory.

The African American population had remained small in Montgomery County. In 1885, of the 97,000 county residents, only 1,763 were African American. While it is believed that Ned Hector was Conshohocken's very first African American resident, thirty-five years after his death in 1870 the borough had 25 African American residents.

By 1881, St. John's African Methodist Episcopal Church, located on the corner of East Eighth Avenue and Harry Street, was constructed to accommodate the growing African American population. In the early 1920s, Reverend Marshall Lee began recruiting members of the black community from the South, where Lee's father had been a slave for many years. Lee found jobs for many of the men at the Alan Wood Steel Company, where Lee himself was employed.

Today, Conshohocken's doors remain open. This former steel town was built by immigrants and continues to welcome anyone, from any country, looking for the American dream. As of 2009, the Irish made up 25 percent of Conshohocken's population, followed by the Italians with 20 percent. The Polish and Germans made up 13 percent of the borough's population while African Americans and English made up 8 percent, with more than a dozen other ethnic groups making up the rest of the town's nine thousand residents.

# THE BRIDGE—MATSON'S FORD, THAT IS

The bridge that spans the Schuylkill River connecting the boroughs of Conshohocken and West Conshohocken goes back before the Revolutionary War, when it was a ford made of large rocks constructed by Peter Matson. In the nearly three hundred years since that ford was built, the two boroughs have shared five different bridges: a covered bridge, the steel bridge that followed, a temporary span, the original concrete arched bridge and, of course, today's modern crossing.

In order to trace the name of the Matsonford Bridge, we go back in history to 1688. Nils (sometimes spelled Neels) Matson and his wife, Margaret, were granted land here. Nils and Margaret had eleven children. Nils's son Peter Matson owned 178 acres along the banks of the Schuylkill River extending from Upper Merion Township into Lower Merion, and he would later purchase additional property. Peter had two sons: Isaac, his eldest son, and Peter Jr. When the elder Peter passed away in December 1778, his son Isaac inherited what was known as the upper plantation, containing 120 acres, formerly owned by Henry Pawling. Peter Jr. inherited the plantation at the ford where his family had lived, containing 178 acres.

Peter Matson Sr. settled along the river in 1741 after securing a deed that described the land as being part of the Manor of Mount Joy and adjoined lands of Thomas Griffith, Thomas and Susan Jones and John Sturgis. Matson

The iron bridge was the second of five bridges built to connect Conshohocken to West Conshohocken. It replaced the covered bridge, opening in 1872, and served the borough until 1919, when construction on the concrete bridge began. The John Woods Manufacturing Company can be seen on the left of the bridge.

built his house on a knoll overlooking the river; the house was demolished in 1920 to make way for the ten-arch concrete bridge.

Peter Matson and his family had strong religious ties and were members of the Friends. The Friends of Plymouth Meeting was established in 1686 and would hold joint services and meetings with Gwynedd, Merion and Radnor Friends. Matson's ties to these organizations unquestionably led to his building of a ford so that meetings could be held on both sides of the river. Matson's Ford was located approximately seventy-five to one hundred yards upriver from today's Matsonford Bridge.

Matson's Ford played a key role during the Revolutionary War in 1777 and again in 1778, and not without damages to Matson's possessions. Matson encountered serious damage to his house and farm thanks to artillery action on May 20, 1778. Matson's Ford played a prominent part for General George Washington's troops, led by twenty-two-year-old General Marquis de Lafayette. Lafayette's soldiers set up a fortress high on the hills above the river and, with cannons and heavy artillery, kept the British from crossing the river, forcing a retreat. Unfortunately, Matson's house was in the line of fire. Following Matson's death in 1778, his estate was one of the largest claimants for the damages wrought principally by the activity of that May 20, 1778 skirmish.

By the early 1830s, members of the Matson family formed a bridge company originally called the President, Manager and Company of the Schuylkill Bridge of Matson's Ford. The name was later shortened to the Matson's Ford Bridge Company (and later renamed the Matsonford Bridge Company). In 1833, a covered bridge was constructed, crossing the river just yards from the Matsons' house. With the building of this bridge, the original Matson's Ford crossing was abandoned. For many years, the rock crossing was very visible, but today no sign of the crossing can be found.

The original covered bridge spanned only the river from bank to bank. It measured 520 feet long and 25 feet wide. The cost of the first bridge was $13,000. A spring freshet in 1839 wiped out the bridge, but it was quickly rebuilt and opened in October 1840. The swollen Schuylkill River claimed the bridge again on September 2, 1850. The bridge was washed downriver to Philadelphia but remained in fairly good condition and was rebuilt again very quickly. In an effort to increase the revenues of the bridge, railroad tracks were installed on the bridge in 1860. Railroad trains were pulled by mules, helping travelers to move their goods—for a fee, of course.

Once he emerged from the covered bridge on the Conshohocken side of the river, the traveler entered a short covered bridge that crossed the canal. It was in between bridges that he stopped to pay a toll.

According to the original minutes reprinted in the *Conshohocken Recorder* newspaper, a sign was posted at both ends of the bridge announcing the fees for the use of the bridge:

*Rate of Tolls Authorized to be taken at the Matsonford Bridge—1838*

*For Every Score of Sheep --------------------6cts*
*For Every Score of Hogs----------------------10 cts*
*For Every Score of Cattle---------------------20cts*
*For Every Horse or Mule----------------------3cts*
*For Every Horse and Rider-------------------4cts*
*For Every Foot Passenger---------------------1ct*
*For Every Sulkey, Chaise or Gig with One Horse or Two Wheels----------------6cts*
*For Every Chariot, Coach, Phaeton or Chaise with Two Horses and Four Wheels--------12 & half cts*
*For Either of the Aforesaid Carriages with Four Horses-----25cts*
*For Every Stage Wagon with Two Horses----------------------12 & half cts*
*For Every Sleigh for Every Horse Drawing the Same----------6 & a quarter cts*
*For Every Sled and for Every Horse Drawing Same-----------4 cts*
*For Every Wagon or Cart per Horse--------------------------5cts*
*Two Oxen to be estimated equal to one horse*
*Marble or all other heavy loads*
*For three tons burden--------------4cts per horse*
*For four tons burden---------------5cts per horse*
*For five tons, 8cts, six tons, 9cts, seven tons, 10cts, up to 12 tons for 15cts*

*No Tolls shall be demanded of any persons, attending Funerals, nor returning from the same. And all persons going to and returning from military parades, going to or returning from church, children going to or returning from school, going to or returning from general elections or walking in military processions.*

The covered bridge fell into disrepair in the late 1860s, and the Matsonford Bridge Company opted for the removal of the covered span and replaced it with a more modern wood and steel, open-air bridge. In 1886, the Matsonford Bridge Company was purchased by Montgomery County, and tolls were abolished.

In early 1916, several trucks had fallen through the wooden planks of the steel bridge. Because of the deteriorating condition of the structure, Montgomery County commissioners assigned four watchmen (costing the county eighty-four dollars per week) to monitor the amount of traffic allowed on the bridge at one time and the weight of the vehicles. Restrictions on the bridge caused many fights with the four guards, one at each end of the bridge for twelve-hour shifts. The speed limit on the bridge was four miles per hour, with tickets handed out, and any truck that looked too heavy was ordered to drive to Norristown to cross the bridge there.

By 1918, plans for a new, more modern concrete bridge were in place, and construction began with the building of the borough's third bridge, a temporary wooden span to be used during the two-plus years of construction of the new bridge. Construction of a temporary bridge made of wood began on November 24, 1919, with workers began driving piles over the canal. The temporary bridge was built some fifty yards upriver from where the concrete structure was to be built.

On December 27, 1919, the first concrete was poured on the West Conshohocken side of the river for a retaining wall. On March 5, 1920, large chunks of ice in the rapidly flowing river washed out the temporary bridge. Two months later, the temporary bridge was in service.

Seeds & Derham Construction was the low bidder for the construction of the bridge, coming in at a total cost of $638,500. The bid also included the removal of ten buildings that would be in the right of way for the new bridge, including the home of Peter Matson located on the West Conshohocken side of the river. Behind the Matson house were two brick homes that were demolished; they had been owned by John Sowers and his brother Monroe. At the corner of Front and Ford Streets was a barbershop owned and operated by Robert Reid. Next to Reid's barbershop was a blacksmith shop, wheelwright buildings and a house, all owned by J. Fred Beaumont. On the Conshohocken side of the river was the old Conshohocken Hotel, once owned and operated by James Wells, whose signature can be found on the Conshohocken incorporation papers. The bridge ticket office once used to collect tolls, the home of the bridge caretaker and one of the first iron mills erected in the borough were also demolished.

When finished, the new bridge spanned the river, canal, three sets of railroad tracks and two roads. The new bridge was twice as wide as the covered bridge, at fifty feet wide (the covered bridge was twenty-five feet wide). When it was built from 1919 to 1921, materials used to create the span included 25,000 cubic yards of concrete, 672 tons of steel, 5,750 square yards of wood block paving, 2,110 square yards of granite, 1,607 square yards of bithulithic, 31,700 barrels of cement, 16,500 tons of sand and 28,700 tons of gravel.

When the bridge opened in 1921, the road surface looked like cobblestone but was actually wooden blocks. The blocks were coated with oil and creosote, and when it rained, the blocks became very slippery like ice and were very dangerous. Within six months, the blocks were removed and a hard surface was installed.

Minnie Harrison, an East Fourth Avenue resident, penned a poem that ran in the *Conshohocken Recorder* in November 1921 pertaining to the opening of the bridge:

> *Across the Schuylkill's rippling tide*
> *A mighty bridge is flung*
> *And it is long and high and wide*
> *And open to the sun.*
>
> *It welds the East unto the West*
> *With strong and fervent tie*
> *And just beneath on either side*
> *The many factories lie.*
>
> *And on the West are glorious hills*
> *With trees and foliage fair*
> *And water from the coldest spring*
> *Azure skies and pure fresh air.*
>
> *And in the vale are many homes*
> *And honest hearts and true*
> *If you're a stranger in the town*
> *We'll gladly welcome you.*
>
> *And there's no fairer valley*
> *Within the land of Penn*
> *Than by the river Schuylkill*
> *With its loyal maids and men.*

The concrete bridge built in 1921 may have been the finest bridge in the nation at that time, but by the 1970s it was in deplorable condition. Major holes started showing up in the sidewalks and the roadbed, and then the railing started to deteriorate. The writing was on the wall. Conshohocken was about to embark on a federal urban renewal project that would take the town from rags to riches, but a new bridge was needed.

A mighty explosion in the spring of 1986 brought the 1921 structure down, and work began on the new $12 million bridge. If you're keeping score, the covered bridge coast nearly $12,000, the 1921 bridge cost a cool $638,500 and in 1987, the fifty-two-foot-wide span cost $12 million; that equates to nearly $1 million for every hundred feet of the bridge. John Capozzi, who was the president of the Conshohocken Chamber of Commerce in 1987, said it best as he spoke from the bridge deck during the grand opening on November 27, 1987: "To us, this is the most important 1,380 feet of road surface in the state of Pennsylvania."

Over the years, two efforts have been made to change the name of the bridge. The first was in 1987, when the Conshohocken Chamber of Commerce suggested that the name be changed to the Conshohocken Bridge. The second attempt came at a West Conshohocken Council meeting in 2000, when veteran John DiRusso proposed changing the name of the bridge to Pearl Harbor Memorial Bridge. While both name changes were taken very seriously, after nearly three centuries, the name remains Matsonford Bridge.

# Part Three

# Industry

## IT ALL STARTED WITH A SHOVEL HEAD

Iron furnaces and forges began operating in this area in the early days of Pennsylvania. Ore was dug out of the ground from a number of locations throughout the area. Thomas Rutter started his forge on Manatawny Creek, at the present Montgomery-Berks County line. He built his forge in 1716, and it became Pennsylvania's first iron industry.

In 1832, James Wood and his son Alan began making steel in a one-room building alongside the Schuylkill Canal in Conshohocken. Nearly a century later, in 1920, the Alan Wood Steel Company employed more than five thousand local residents and produced more than 8 percent of the nation's output of steel.

It all started when James Wood established a "smithy" near Hickorytown (formerly known as Pigeontown) more than ninety years after Rutter started his forge. Wood became known as a "black and white" smith because in addition to the ordinary work of the blacksmith, he also made kitchen or domestic wares.

James Wood was the grandson of a Dublin Quaker immigrant named James who fled to America in 1725 and settled in Gwynedd. James, the grandson, was born on October 23, 1771, on a farm in Montgomery County, near Narcissa or Five Points. Wood recalled that General George Washington was a guest at the Wood home in 1777, when seven-year-old James sat on the knee of General Washington, who was on his way to Valley Forge.

Workers at the Alan Wood Steel plant can be seen working during the company's heyday in the 1920s. In 1920, Alan Wood Steel was producing more than 8 percent of the nation's output of steel. The Alan Wood Company opened in Conshohocken in 1832 and closed in 1977.

An agreement between James and Alan effective on January 1, 1832, resulted in the erection of a water mill for rolling iron at Conshohocken. Wood's iron mill was located along the canal owned by the Schuylkill Navigation Company. The location included a ground rent of twenty-five cents per running foot yearly. The Schuylkill Navigation Company also contracted to supply "900 square inches of water at an annual rent of $1,000."

When production began on May 5, 1832, steel was processed to make shovel plates. Wood developed an early patent on steel shovel heads. In 1835, the Woods expanded their operation by building a three-story shovel factory at the west end of the mill.

The company remained strong during the country's Great Depression and worked in the war effort for the government during the 1940s. Following the war, a recapitalization plan was introduced in 1948 and was the company's first step in modernizing in nearly three decades. This resulted in major improvements in 1953 and '54, when multimillion-dollar improvements were made and new equipment was installed. By 1956, more than $56 million had been spent to upgrade the plant. In the early 1960s, the most sophisticated oxygen furnace was installed at a cost of $37 million. The company was forced to spend millions more in the early 1970s for improvements and pollution control programs.

The money spent during the company's final thirty years was a tremendous burden. The Wood company was unable to regain its hold on the steel industry as the large contracts were being purchased from overseas competitors at cheaper prices. Despite recording record sales of $98 million in 1969, the company filed for bankruptcy on June 10, 1977.

After more than 145 years, the steel mill fell silent. More than 2,500 employees found themselves unemployed. The company was paying out more than $1 million annually to Conshohocken and Plymouth Township in taxes, so the closure of the plant crippled the borough of Conshohocken. In later years, Lukens's Steel would occupy a small part of the Alan Wood Steel Company site, but it was never to be returned to the 5,000 employees who once gutted out a living making steel.

An old *Philadelphia Inquirer* writer named Edgar Williams would sometimes remind his readers of the Alan Wood Steel Company with small anecdotes in his column like, "Just once more let people in the Conshohocken area see the 'Connaughttown' (pronounced Cunneytown) Moon, the glow that lit up the night sky whenever slag was dumped at night at the old Alan Wood Steel Company plant."

# JOHN ELWOOD LEE, WHAT A MAN

John Elwood Lee was born in Conshohocken on November 15, 1860, to Bradford Adams Lee and Sarah A. Raysor. John's father worked more than thirty-five years for the Schuylkill Iron Works and the J. Wood & Brothers rolling mill. Before John Elwood turned forty years old, he would be a multimillionaire, with his products known throughout the world, and one of the most respected businessmen in the country.

Upon Lee's graduation from Conshohocken High School in 1879, Charles Heber Clark landed him a job with William Snowden and Company. Snowden's company manufactured surgical instruments in Philadelphia. On April 12, 1882, young Lee married Jennie W. Cleaver (together they would have four children), and a year later, he decided to leave the Snowden Company and strike out on his own.

At the age of twenty-three, he decided to start his own business with a cash capital of $28.35. Lee was very savvy, and in the attic of his parents' house on Seventh Avenue, with his mother's sewing machine, he started what would become the second leading manufacturer of surgical supplies in the country.

Lee adapted the sewing machine for the purpose of rolling of bandages and reeling surgeons' silk. His purpose in the beginning was to produce a standard ligature material for surgeons. In just a few months, his growing business required larger quarters. Lee constructed a two-story building in his parents' backyard, and with the extra working space, he added more products.

In 1888, the J. Elwood Lee Company was incorporated. The original members of the company included Charles Heber Clark (Lee's Sunday school teacher) as president of the organization; Charles Lukens, vice-president; J. Elwood Lee, treasurer, secretary and general manager; and Alan Wood Jr., Howard Wood and Conrad B. Lee on the board of directors. Conrad Lee passed away less than ten years later, and Frank R. Jones joined the board of directors. Later that year, in 1888, the company established a factory for the manufacture of woven catheters, the first and only factory in America at that time to produce such a product.

In November 1893, the Lee Company participated in the 1893 World's Columbian Exposition and was presented with the exposition's five highest awards, including;

*For Woven Flexible Catheters*
*For Surgeons' Silk Ligatures*
*For Lee's Metallic Splints*
*For Antiseptic Gauze in Glass Containers*
*For General Hospital Supplies*

While Lee's Surgical Works had been for years acknowledged by many leading surgeons, supply houses and hospitals throughout America, the Exposition Awards brought the Lee Company attention from around the world.

Lee started buying out other small surgical supply companies, starting with Grosvenor & Richards, J.C. De La Cour, John Parker Manufacturing Company and a half dozen others. With all the acquisitions, by 1905 the J. Elwood Lee Company consisted of seventeen buildings located on East Eighth Avenue and Harry Street. (Part of Lee factory still stands today.) The factory covered more than five acres of floor space and employed more than five hundred Conshohocken residents.

# Industry

The Lee Company was the second leading manufacturer of surgical supplies in the country, only behind Johnson & Johnson from New Brunswick, New Jersey. Eventually, the two companies merged, and Mr. Lee became the executive vice-president of the Johnson & Johnson Company.

By 1908, the automobile had surfaced as a rich man's toy, and Lee was fascinated with the rubber tires. He felt that improvements could be made by utilizing the knowledge he had acquired of rubber and its characteristics in the manufacture of such goods as surgical tubing and rubber gloves. Lee had the wisdom of rubber, the engineers and the resources to make tires.

By 1909, plans were underway for Lee to construct a tire factory. He purchased twenty-six acres from the Righter family in the Spring Mill section of town on the corner of Hector Street and North Lane, and by 1910, JELCO Tires was up and running. JELCO, a Lee trademark that had appeared on all his pharmaceutical supplies, stood for "John Elwood Lee Company."

When Lee discussed supplying Henry Ford tires for his cars rolling off the assembly line in Detroit, Michigan, his friend pointed out to Lee that printing the JELCO trademark on the side of his tires would make the public skeptical of riding on tires that sounded soft, as in "jelly." It was then that Lee made the decision that would make his tire company famous all over the world with his trademark "Lee of Conshohocken" trademark.

Lee's first major breakthrough in the tire factory was his famous "Puncture Proof Tire." His second would change the course of tire making throughout the world. Charles Goodyear tire factory introduced the vulcanization of rubber, allowing us to shape rubber products for many different uses. In 1912, Lee started to experiment with the possibilities from the use of vanadium in rubber. A year later, in September 1913, vanadium rubber proved beyond a shadow of a doubt that Lee could produce the cheapest rubber available. Treated with the vanadium process, it was twice as durable as the finest rubber on the market.

As the tire factory started producing tires at a rate of 2,500 per day, Lee and his wife, Jennie, lived in a modest house located at Eighth Avenue and Fayette Street. In May 1893, Lee awarded a contract to Alexander Martin and Son to erect a handsome pointed stone mansion on the property Lee had purchased. The three-story, twenty-three-room mansion, when completed, was a beautiful building located just one block from his surgical supply business and a block and a half from his parents' home. The mansion was called Leeland and had a state-of-the-art carriage house, complete with a bowling alley, swimming pool and gym. (Lee was an avid sportsman.) Lee also built a golf course behind the mansion on property he owned, located between Seventh and Twelfth Avenues from Forrest Street down to Wood Street.

John Elwood Lee passed away on the evening of April 8, 1914. He was fifty-four years old. His wife, Jennie, lived until 1945.

Lee Tires of Conshohocken would go on making tires for the next half century until a bitter strike by the union employees kept the doors closed for two years, from 1963 to 1965. When the plant reopened in 1965, Goodyear exercised its right to purchase the company. All of Lee's assets, trade names, patents, tires and tubes were now property of Goodyear.

The Hector Street factory continued to make tires under Goodyear ownership, and in 1974, a milestone was reached at the Lee plant when the twenty-five millionth tire was produced. Three years later, the plant surpassed thirty-six million tires. In the late 1970s, Goodyear executives decided the tire factory was outdated, and in 1979, the decision was made to close the plant for good. On February 10, 1980, the last tires were made at the Spring Mill plant. The closing was due largely to the declining market for bias ply tires, caused primarily by the increased popularity of radial tires, many of which were produced overseas.

# NEWTON AND HERVEY, THE WALKER BROTHERS

When you say the name Walker Brothers, one might think of an American pop group formed in 1964 that sang songs like "The Sun Ain't Gonna Shine Anymore" or "Make It Easy on Yourself." But in Conshohocken, if you say "Walker Brothers," most old-timers would tell you about a couple of brothers who formed the Walker Brothers of Conshohocken and became the leading manufactures of under-floor electric distribution systems in the country.

The Walker brothers, Hervey and Newton, founded the company in 1912 and, by 1958, employed more than 650 production workers and more than 200 administrative employees, most of whom were Conshohocken residents. The company operated on eighteen acres of prime riverfront property, much of it later purchased by Quaker Chemical.

Early contracts for Walker Brothers included the designing and installation of switchboards for the United States naval vessels, notably the USS *Wyoming*. The *Wyoming* was a battleship weighing twenty-seven thousand tons and was built at the William Cramp and Sons Shipyard in Philadelphia and commissioned in 1912 at League Island Navy Yard. It was for a time the flagship of the Atlantic Fleet's commander-in-chief, Rear Admiral Charles J. Badger. Badger served with the fleet during World War I and was present at the surrender of the German Grand Fleet off May Island on November 20, 1918.

By the early 1920s, Walker Brothers had begun making and installing under-floor electrical distribution systems and, in 1923, landed its first installation at the Jefferson Standard Building of Greensboro, North Carolina. Once Walker installed the system in that first building, the company had trouble keeping up with production, as it began work on buildings such as the United States Supreme Court Building in Washington, D.C., the Equitable Assurance Building in New York, the Inquirer Building in Philadelphia, the H.J. Reynolds Tobacco Building in Winston-Salem, North Carolina, several buildings on Wall Street and dozens more. In later years, Walker installations included heavy power cables vital to space satellite launchings at Cape Canaveral, Florida, and an under-floor wiring system in the White House Oval Office, transmitting reports of nuclear events to the president of the United States of America.

By the mid-1920s, Walker Brothers realized that it needed a suburban location that would provide space for continued expansion. Hervey pointed out an old abandoned terra cotta pottery factory site in the Spring Mill section of Montgomery County. Newton was unimpressed with the property, but Hervey pointed out the rich history of the area, not to mention two railroads—the Pennsylvania and Reading lines—running right past the property, the river and canal behind the property and finished roadways for overland shipping and transportation. Newton also pointed out the successful businesses just across the tracks, including the Lee Tire and Rubber Company and, just up the Schuylkill River, Alan Wood Steel Company, operating at that point for nearly a century.

On June 5, 1926, Walker Brothers officially purchased the property from George N. Witherspoon and his wife, Jean, of Hendersonville, North Carolina. The riverfront property that had been known as the old Moreland Clay Works was purchased for a total price of $16,715.88, with an adjoining fifty-foot lot bought for $1,621.00.

Years later, when Walker Brothers of Conshohocken Company became the biggest manufacturer of underground electric cables in the country, Hervey turned his attention to civic-minded projects. In March 1945, the Walkers founded the Conshohocken Business Association with 62 charter members. Newton spearheaded the purchase of Leeland, the former home of John Elwood Lee, located on the corner of Eighth Avenue and Fayette Street, and turned the property into a centrally located meeting place. By the early 1950s, more than 150 local business executives and industrial men would meet at Leeland, set up as a luncheonette to discuss routine problems pertaining to production, sales, labor and current economic situations and outlooks.

In 1953, after more than three years of Newton raising money for the Conshohocken Community Chest for the purpose of building a youth center called the Fellowship House (a name given by Newton Walker), the community center opened its door with Newton presiding. The Fellowship House opened at Christmastime in 1953 at a grand building cost of $225,000, most of it donated by Walker Brothers or fundraising undertaken by Newton.

In 1958, following a fire at the Harry Street School, the borough was in financial straits and unable to rebuild the school. It was Hervey to the rescue—he drafted the plans and laid out a good portion of the funds to rebuild a modern school, renamed Hervey S. Walker Elementary School. In 1957, a group of businessmen founded the Leeland Foundation, with Albert A. Garthwaite Sr. as president and Hervey S. Walker as one of the founders. The Leeland Foundation still gives out grants and supports Conshohocken today.

Hervey S. Walker never lived in Conshohocken; in fact, he lived six miles from the town in Haverford. He passed away in September 1958 in Atlantic City. Many people never knew what the "S." stood for in his name; it was Stricker, Hervey Stricker Walker.

## THE QUAKER CHEMICAL STORY

Quaker Chemical had very humble beginnings when Emil Niessen, a German-born chemist who had been a salesman for a chemical company, began his business on December 13, 1918. Niessen started his business on the second floor of an old factory that was located on the berm bank between the canal and the Schuylkill River. The John Wood Manufacturing Company would later expand and occupy the site.

Niessen manufactured oil products and lubrications for the textile industries. He called his company Quaker Oil Products. By 1927, Emil Niessen had moved the company to its present location, an old glass factory on the border of Conshohocken and Whitemarsh Township along East

Hector Street. As the nation was headed into a depression, an offer came to sell the company. Mr. Niessen was only too happy to sell to brothers D.J. and L. Osmond Benoliel, while Niessen retained part ownership. By 1930, the firm incorporated as Quaker Chemical Products Company and consisted of twenty employees, including laborers, two chemists and nine office employees. The nation felt the full impact of the Depression by the end of 1930. Many local factories were working four-day workweeks, but Quaker Chemical Products Company managed to go over $200,000 in sales for the year.

Over the next twenty years, Quaker expanded, opening plants in Wilmington, Chicago and Detroit. The postwar years helped stimulate Quaker's business with the growing automobile industry and the popularity of household appliances. By 1953, Quaker Chemical had posted more than $10 million in sales.

In April 1951, a massive explosion at Quaker set the company back but not out. The explosion caused a fire that gutted most of the main production plant, causing more than $400,000 in damages. The employees worked around the clock to rebuild the plant in something of a record time. Company executives were pleased when the production lines were back in full force and not a single customer was lost.

Today, the Quaker Chemical Company is still headquartered in Conshohocken, with regional headquarter locations in China, Brazil, Shanghai, Rio de Janeiro and the Netherlands. From $200,000 in sales back in 1930 to a $581.6 million company today, Quaker continues its commitment to excellence for its customers.

Quaker Chemical treated its customers the way it has treated the Conshohocken community for more than ninety years. Along with the Walker brothers, the Benoliel family contributed much to the building and maintenance of the Conshohocken Fellowship House. Peter Benoliel, chairman of the board for many years, took a keen interest in the Fellowship House and the development of Conshohocken's youngsters, participating in many events throughout the years. The Quaker Chemical Company has never failed to support Conshohocken, and Quaker is currently helping many communities not only throughout this country but around the world as well.

# ALAN C. HALE, ALMOST A CENTURY

The story of Hale Pumps of Conshohocken can be traced to Wayne, Pennsylvania. In 1906, the Radnor Fire Company purchased a new state-of-the-art motorized fire pumper, the first in America. Radnor firefighters Jan Wendell and Charlie Young would often take the horseless fire carriage to the Hale Knox Motor Company garage for repairs. Alan C. Hale, who owned the garage, was also an active firefighter with the Radnor squad. Hale shared a common interest with Wendell and Young to make firefighting equipment more efficient, especially the horseless carriage and its pumping capacity of water to extinguish fires.

The three dedicated firefighters developed an interest in the new motorized fire carriage and strongly believed improvements could be made on both the truck and pump that would provide better fire protection to the community. The three men formed a partnership and set up shop at the Hale Knox garage, making fire engine pumps. The company would be known as the Hale Motor Company.

By 1914, a military conflict was raging overseas, and before it was over the conflict would become known as World War I and involve most of the world's great powers. In that same year, the three partners came up with a new pump for firefighting called Young Giant and, shortly thereafter, got its first test. The bronze body pump was mounted on a secondhand simplex chassis, and on December 30, 1914, the Young Giant was called out to fight a fire at the Wayne Opera House.

Fire companies from throughout Philadelphia and Montgomery County took notice when the Young Giant pumped water for six straight hours until the fire was extinguished. The George Clay Fire Company of West Conshohocken was so impressed with the truck and pump that the company purchased the truck and used it for more than ten years before purchasing another Hale truck. The Hale Motor Company all of a sudden had trouble keeping up with the demand for the trucks and pumps. By 1917, it was time to move to Conshohocken.

The Hale Motor Company of Wayne purchased a plot of ground on Spring Mill Avenue near Eighth Avenue from C.A. Desimone. The company awarded a contract to Burns and Desimone for the erection of a one-story brick building forty by ninety-six feet. The Hale Motor Company was already building fire pumps and trucks for Plymouth Fire Company, Conshohocken Fire Company No. 2 and George Clay Fire Company, among others. The new plant was dedicated to the building of pumps and would employ about fifteen local skilled mechanics. It was at this time that the partnership was incorporated, becoming Hale Fire Pump Company. Alan C. Hale was the company's first president and treasurer, and Wendell and Young were members of the board of directors.

By 1924, Alan Hale had resigned from the pump company to concentrate on his garage business. Hale had a love of the automobile and wanted to devote more time to the auto industry. E.J. Wendell took over as president and general manager of the Hale Fire Pump Company, and in 1924, the Conshohocken plant quadrupled in size. Hale would continue to expand its operations in the borough for the next fifty years.

In 1952, Hale purchased seven acres of land to build a new plant on Washington Street at the foot of Jones Street, in an area formerly known as "the Meadow." The Meadow served the borough as a baseball field for close to seventy-five years.

In 1974, Hale opened a "clean air" foundry, also located on Washington Street, that featured both induction and gas-melting furnaces used by gas and electric. The thirty-four-thousand-square-foot foundry cast pump parts in iron, aluminum and brass. In that same year, the company also broke ground for the second phase for a new sixteen-thousand-square-foot air-conditioned machine shop. With the addition of the foundry, the company employed as many as 250 union employees by the mid-1970s.

The Hale Fire Pump Company started with 3 men and a fire pump back in 1914; by 1922, 24 employees found full-time work with the company. By 1954, a total of 240 employees were collecting paychecks from Hale, and by the mid-1970s, more than 500 employees, including office personnel, enjoyed employment with the Conshohocken firm.

Generations of families have realized the American dream working at the Hale Fire Pump Company, and today Hale Products Inc., with products and production plants throughout the world, continues to employ Conshohocken residents while servicing the continent with the best firefighting equipment in the world.

## And There's More

Cigar, brewery, ice cream and casket companies were all part of Conshohocken's job market at one time or another. In 1928, the Bobrow brothers opened up their cigar factory, called Bobrow Brothers Cigar Manufactures. The cigar factory was a three-story building located on the corner of Hector and Apple Streets.

The Crystal Spring Brewing Company was located on the southwest corner of Hector and Jones Streets. F.A. Loeba started the business in 1898, and two years later, it became the Crystal Spring Brewing Company. The company was short-lived, closing its doors in 1902. The building for many years was occupied by the Acme Saw Company, owned by the Capozzi family, and is currently a condominium complex. Also around the turn of the twentieth century was the Leibert and Obert Brewing Company, once located on the canal bank. The company also had a cold storage building, where it stored kegs of beer. According to newspaper accounts in 1910, the cold storage building was also the site of weekend drinking get-togethers for the young men about town.

In 1919, I.D. Shaffer leased his planing mill located at Elm and Maple Streets to the newly organized Conshohocken Burial Casket Company. The casket company was unable to sell to any of the local undertakers for the first four weeks, as it had backorders promised.

The Harvey Ice Cream Company was opened in 1929 by Michael J. Harvey. The Eleventh Avenue resident built a two-story ice cream factory at the corner of Twelfth and Maple Streets and purchased the most modern ice cream–making equipment available.

Vistex Brothers out of New York opened a yarn plant in 1929 that would employ more than seventy Conshohocken residents. In 1889, Stanley Lee had his cotton factory in full operation, and in that same year, James and Lawrence Ogden operated a woolen factory. Textile mills employed thousands of residents on both sides of the river for many years, including Superior Knitting Mill, Rambo & Regar Knitting Mill and J&S Lees Textile Mill. Aramink Carpet Mills, owned by James Hall, began in West Conshohocken in 1881 and employed more than fifty residents. The J.N. Susskind Company purchased the old Lee Surgical Supply factory at Eighth Avenue and Harry Street and for many decades manufactured military clothing.

In January 1918, the Ford & Kendig Company of Philadelphia announced the purchase of seven and a half acres from R.V. Mattison of Ambler. The ground was located on Washington Street and was the former site of the Longmead Iron Company. Ford & Kendig was one of the best known manufacturers engaged in the iron pipe and steam specialties business. The firm was incorporated in March 1888 by partners Alfred E. Ford and John Kendig, and the two established their business at 712 Filbert Street in Philadelphia. Within the first year in Conshohocken, nearly 150 residents were employed for the pipe-making business. By 1930, the company announced an expansion that would increase the workforce by another 150 employees to work in the foundry and warehouse. The Ford & Kendig Company ceased operations in the 1980s, and the site is currently one of many office buildings constructed by O'Neill Properties, owned by Brian O'Neill.

Frank Carlile and Leon Doughty were high school buddies, and in their senior year of high school in 1906, the two envisioned a future where the new technology of electricity would power the nation into a new century. By 1912, the two friends had set up a small battery plant in Conshohocken called Carlile and Doughty Batteries, later shortened to C&D Batteries. C&D Batteries operated out of Conshohocken for nearly ninety years before moving its headquarters to Blue Bell, Pennsylvania. The battery company took off in Conshohocken, and by the Second World War, it met the challenges by developing industrial batteries. The company stayed on top of the industry and never failed to expand with the changing demands of technology. Today, C&D Technologies has locations throughout the world, including Mexico, England, Canada, China and several locations in the United States. For more than a century, C&D Technologies has followed the lead of Carlile and Doughty by continuing to meet the technological challenges of the future.

Although we can't mention the hundreds of companies that have had a chapter in the borough's history, here's a list of some of the old—and not so old—factories, mills, companies and other places where Conshohockenites have earned a living for their families.

A few were founded in the 1800s: Longmead Iron Works, 1882; Plymouth Rolling Mill, 1881; H.C. Jones Company, 1880–1950; Colwell's Furnace, 1866; Merion Furnace, 1866; Spring Mill Terra Cotta Works, 1898; Schuylkill Iron Works, 1898; Schuylkill Woolen Mills, 1898; Poulterer & Co. Iron & Steel & Machinery, 1898; A.L. Miller & Co. Planing Mill, 1898; Albion Print Works, 1871; Joseph Whitton Woolen Mills, 1871; John O'Brien Brick Yard, 1871; George Tracy Brick Yard, 1871; George S. Yerks Planing Mill, 1871; Walter Cresson and Brother Saw Factory, 1889; Jacoby & Company Marble Yard and Saw Mill, 1889; Farr & Kinzie Furnace, 1835; Merion and Elizabeth Furnaces and Merion Iron Company in West Conshohocken, 1847; Plymouth Furnaces, 1845; W.C. Hamilton & Sons, 1856; and Merion Worsted Mills, 1891.

A few industries some of us just might remember founded in the 1900s include: the Bentley-Harris Manufacturing Co., 1924; Philip Carey Manufacturing Co., 1902; Coopers Creek Chemical Co., 1938; Empress Hosiery Co., 1937; Flexton Inc., 1946; Francis L. Freas Glass Works, 1905;

Glassine Paper Co., 1925; Graeber Machine Works, 1927; Gray's Ferry Brick Company, 1942 (Gray's Ferry Brick Company was located in the former Harrison mansion once located at the corner of Seventh Avenue and Fayette Street, currently the CVS Pharmacy); Kimble Glass Co., 1910; E.J. Levino & Co., 1916; Moser Glass Works, 1914; Philadelphia Steel & Iron Co., 1929; Philadelphia Uniform Co., 1903; Reilly-Whitman-Walton Co., 1923; Tompkins Rubber Co., 1938; United Pattern Co., 1939; Valley Forge Cement Co., 1927; Yergey Peanut Co., 1936; Chrome Alloy Products Inc., 1929; No-Gum Products Co., 1918; and Getz-There Soap Laundry Company, opening in 1908 and employing more than fifty residents. The laundry business was operated out of the old Martin Building once located on Hector Street.

In 1937, the Marsden Glass Corporation moved to Conshohocken following seventeen years of production in Ambler. J.E. Marsden was the owner of the glass company that manufactured the glass vacuum—type coffee maker, for which Mr. Marsden held the patent. The plant was located on the property located at Elm and Ash Streets and employed seventy-five residents.

In December 1930, a new industry began operation in the old Miller Planing Mill owned at that time by C.B. Daring Millwork Company, once located at Elm and Poplar Streets. The construction of miniature golf courses for home use would be manufactured with the help of eight to ten employees. Keep in mind that in 1930, Conshohocken had four public miniature golf courses, and an in-home miniature golf course was very popular at the time. The four public miniature golf courses were the Washita Indoor Course, once located at Sixth Avenue and Harry Street; the Rock Garden Golf Course, located at Sixteenth and Fayette Streets; the Conshohocken Junior Golf Course, run by Henry Feingold and located at Twelfth Avenue and Wood Street; and Fayette Street Junior Golf Course, located at Twelfth and Fayette Streets.

# Part Four

# The Uniforms: Police, Firemen and Military

## POLICE

### *Conshy, Times Were Tough*

In 1850, when Conshohocken incorporated as a borough, the village had a mere 727 residents and very little, if any, criminal activity. Twenty years later, the young borough was laying down the foundation for becoming a major industrial town. The iron- and millworkers were a young, rough bunch who, upon being paid on Saturday mornings, found themselves in one or more of the local taverns for an afternoon of relaxation. By early evening, the overcrowded bars, some with dirt floors, became a crush of loud voices, rattling bottles and the smell of stale beer.

Generally, the conversations were jovial, and all too often the ironworkers would get to bragging about their abilities as workers. More than once the townspeople were heard saying that "more iron was made in the saloons on Saturday night than made at the mills during the week." Of course, all of their differences were settled outside.

The workers came from Fulton's two furnaces in Conshohocken and Moorehead's two furnaces in West Conshohocken, and the workers from Spring Mill furnaces were always involved in the weekly fisticuffs, as were the employees from the furnace at Matsunk—now Swedeland—and the mighty ironworkers of Alan Wood. As the industries grew, so did the taverns and saloons, and by 1870, the Saturday night get-togethers also included the quarry workers from Whitemarsh, the lime burners from Plymouth and, of course, the steel workers from Connaughtown.

The Conshohocken Police Department was formed in the early 1870s and was already more than fifty years old when this photo was taken in the mid-1920s. The four-man police force, led by Chief William Heald (standing in the back on the right), was made up of Samuel Himes, Daniel Donovan and Frank Jacquot. Burgess John Hampton is standing in the back on the left. This photograph was taken outside the police lockup once located on West Hector Street.

Eventually, the company workers formed themselves into company gangs. There were the Connaughtowners, the Guineatowners and the Pikers. Just outside of the borough were the Hickerytowners and the Limeburners from Plymouth. Adding to the rowdiness of the Saturday night drinking parties were the boatmen who worked and traveled along the canal, who tied up their boats on Saturday afternoons until they were sober enough to unhitch the boats on or about Monday morning. The town residents also had to contend with workers from the freight trains as well as the free travelers of the trains known as hobos.

Residents who lived in certain parts of town had trouble traveling to other parts of town because the gang mentality transferred to all parts of the community. West Elm Street became known throughout the borough as "the Bowery" and was a very rough stretch of real estate to pass through, especially when an outsider—particularly one from Connaughtown—attempted to make his way through the Bowery. As stated earlier, Lower

Maple Street was known as Cork Row, named for the Irish section of town, long before Italians started moving into the borough along Maple Street and Cork Row eventually became known as Little Italy.

By 1871, borough officials were under a lot of pressure from the residents to stop the lawlessness and hire a sheriff or policeman. Borough records show that the town was paying fifty dollars per month for two men in 1871 for part-time police service. The borough hired a constable before hiring any police officers. George McGonigle was hired as constable in 1871 and held the post until 1873. John Stemple, known as "Jacky," and Michael Wills, who owned and operated a cigar store on Elm Street for many years, wore civilian clothing with badges as an emblem of authority. Too often, the two part-time officers were not taken seriously, and they were always outnumbered on Saturday nights, forcing the hiring of a full-time police officer.

## Jack Harrold, Conshy's First Cop

Conshohocken Borough Council honored the request of Burgess William Hallowell, and in March 1873, Jack Harrold was appointed as the borough's first full-time policeman at a salary of forty dollars per month. During Harrold's first year serving as a policeman, he was standing on the corner at Fayette and Hector Streets in front of the newly formed First National Bank of Conshohocken. While Harrold was on duty at two o'clock in the morning, a man whose identity was never discovered stood on the opposite side of the street at what was then known as Saylor's Corner. The unidentified man fired three shots at Officer Harrold from a revolver; one of the bullets grazed his shoulder. Officer Harrold, unfazed, chased the man down Fayette Street, past the canal and lost sight of him along the railroad tracks.

Part of Harrold's duties was to light and extinguish the gas street lamps. A single-room jail cell was set up along the Pennsylvania Railroad, and when Harrold would have more than one man in the cell, especially on a Saturday night, the men would continue their fight or start a new one with a fellow inmate. Harrold was often forced to let one prisoner go to prevent a jail cell fight.

Jack Harrold served the borough as a policeman for four years until 1877. Harrold was an amazing individual, as he later served on town council on and off from 1883 until 1922. He was an outstanding baseball player and played on the borough's very first official ball club, called the Nerve of Conshohocken. He later built one of the town's finest hotels of the day on West Elm Street, later known as Zalik's Hotel. Harrold would often entertain his hotel guests as an accomplished violin player, accompanied by his son Donald "Doc" at the piano. Harrold was also a boxer and trained several great boxers of the day, including James J. Corbett. Harrold was in Corbett's corner when he defeated the great John L. Sullivan in twenty-one rounds for the heavyweight title in New Orleans on September 7, 1892.

Harrold wasn't the only police officer in 1873, although he was the only full-time officer. John Field and Joseph Griffith worked as part-time police officers, making twenty-five dollars per month.

## *Police Chiefs and a Few Good Cops*

In 1875, the borough leaders recognized the need for a proper police lockup with at least two jail cells, and later two more cells were added. The borough purchased a lot of ground next to the Washington Fire House on the corner

Francis "Bunny" Blake was sworn in as a Conshohocken police officer in July 1929 and served as a borough policeman for twenty-five years, including a stint as chief from 1934 to 1938. Blake was also a professional boxer and fought 143 professional fights, including a fight with champion Tommy Loughran.

of West Hector and Forrest Streets. The borough still operated with one full-time police officer and two part-time officers.

In 1876, Henry Stemple was appointed as a full-time police officer by Burgess William Summers, the retired grocer. Big, good-natured Stemple had been a teamster by occupation previous to his becoming a policeman, being engaged in the hauling of iron ore from the mines in Plymouth Township to the Fulton furnaces in Conshohocken. Stemple enjoyed his job as a teamster and was a very skillful driver who often drove a team of seven to nine horses. Stemple served as a policeman for seven years and resigned due to ill health; he later died of pulmonary infection.

By 1889, the force had begun to grow, and policemen were appointed for terms of one year by members of council and confirmed by the burgess. In 1889, Michael McCaul was appointed as captain, William Morris was the policeman for the First Ward, Andrew McFeeters was the officer of the Second Ward and Michael J. O'Brien patrolled the Third Ward. By 1895, the borough police budget had swelled to $2,500 per year.

In 1897, William Heald was hired to serve with John Maconachy and John Greer. Heald would later become the borough's second chief of police. In 1902, James Courduff was assigned to the force to serve with officers Daniel Hastings, Charles Holland and Heald. James Courduff became the borough's first chief of police. Following retirement, he passed away in Ocean City, New Jersey, in 1929 at the age of sixty-nine.

In 1907, members of the borough council met to discuss a pay raise for the police. Members of the police force were seeking a ten-dollar-per-month raise, looking to bump their monthly salary to seventy dollars for a sixty-hour workweek.

Salaries for members of the police force continued to grow, and by 1924, Conshohocken's newly appointed Chief of Police William Heald received $125 per month for overseeing a four-man police department that included Daniel Donovan and Officer Harrington. Patrolmen were pulling down a cool $100 per month for six days per workweek.

After more than thirty-two years as a Conshohocken policeman, Chief William Heald died of a heart attack in 1928 and was replaced by longtime police officer Daniel Donovan. Donovan stepped into Herald's salary, now up to $1,800 annually. Donovan held the chief's position until his death in 1934.

Following Donovan's death, one of Conshohocken's most colorful characters was appointed chief. Francis "Bunny" Blake, who was born in 1900, was sworn in as a police officer in July 1929. Although he only served for four years as chief, he went on to serve more than twenty years as a policeman. Bunny was also a professional boxer, fighting more than 143 professional fights, including a fight with champion Tommy Loughran.

Walter Phipps Sr. became the borough's fifth chief of police in 1938 and served as a policeman for more than thirty years before retiring in 1959. A few of the more colorful policemen who served during the late 1920s and 1930s included Mike Bosco, Frank Jacquot, Samuel Himes, Henry Williams, Frank Stalone, Harry Snear, William P. Donovan and Ezekiel Kirkpatrick, just to name a few.

A little bit of police business back in 1937 included borough officials accepting the bid of E.F. Moore Chevrolet to furnish a Chevrolet Master Coach for use by the police at a price of $208.50. The old police car was used as a trade-in. Even back then, our borough leaders spared no expense for the police department.

In 1943, Councilman Kelly voted to increase the police salary raise percentage from 5 percent to 10 percent. All council voted in favor of the additional raise. After all, the police department—including Chief of Police Walter Phipps and officers Francis "Bunny" Blake, Louis Haushalter, Harry Snear and Frank Stalone—had just captured a gang of thieves. The only problem with the raise, according to Solicitor Arnold Forrest, was that it was illegal, as the budget had already been adopted by the taxpayers. The additional 5 percent raise was later stripped.

In 1944, that new police car purchased in 1937 was in a slight accident when it rear-ended a fire truck on the way back from a field fire. The police department was without a police car for more than two months. Fortunately, three of the borough's policemen had their own transportation, but the other three officers were left to capture the bad guys on foot.

In 1958, borough leaders managed to go one step further with a police department blunder than they had in 1943 when they decided to relieve Walter Phipps of his duty as chief of police. Council voted that all policemen with twenty years of service and who were sixty years old would be forced to retire with a handsome payment of fifty dollars per week. Chief Phipps was removed, and later reinstated, before retiring on his own.

Police pay was again the hot topic in 1960, when Chief of Police Charles Marwood was granted a raise, giving him $6,000 per year. Other officers in 1960—including Ray Alexander, Francis Blake, Matt Doughtery, John Boccella and Harrison M. "Tank" Langley, just to name a few—were pulling down $5,000 per year. In 1961, Sergeant Francis "Bunny" Blake retired after serving more than thirty-two years as a Conshohocken policeman, and in

1962 William "Pat" Donovan retired after serving more than twenty-five years on the department.

By 1964, town council had grown out of the borough offices located on the corner of Hector and Forrest Streets. The combined borough hall and police station purchased in 1875 was antiquated with the four small cells; in 1875, the police force had consisted of one full-time officer and two-part time cops. By 1965, the department had swelled to eleven officers, including Samuel Cardamone, Adam Pagliaro, George Bland, Robert Watson, Frank Charlesworth, Carmen Canale and Jesse Zadroga. These officers were the benefactors of the new police station purchased by the borough located on the corner of Eighth Avenue and Forrest Street. One side note about the new police station was that the old jail cells were removed from the Forrest Street police station and incorporated into the new station, and they are still in use today.

In 1987, the police department had received a new contract giving them a 4 percent raise, followed by a 2 percent raise in 1988. The agreement would raise the starting pay of a police officer from $19,472.00 to $19,861.97. The maximum salary for sergeants would be $27,586.00, an increase of $541.00 per year. Police officers who served during the 1980s included Frank Charlesworth, Paul Price, John Ellam, George Metz, Ed Williamson, Ron Kilbride, Francis Ruggiero, Tony Santoro, Michael Orler and Adam Pagliaro, just to name a few.

There have been at least eleven Conshohocken police chiefs in the nearly 140-year history of the department.

| James Courduff | borough's first chief of police |
|---|---|
| Henry Hollands | chief in 1886 and 1887, sometime before and after |
| William Heald | chief, 1924–28 |
| Daniel Donovan | chief, 1928–34 |
| Francis "Bunny" Blake | chief, 1934–38 |
| Walter Phipps Sr. | chief, 1938–58 |
| Charles Marwood | chief, 1959–unknown |
| Raymond Alexander | chief |
| Adam Pagliaro | chief, unknown–1993 |
| James Doughtery | chief, 1994–2009 |
| Michael Orler | chief, 2009–present |

## Headlines and a Few Good Stories

A few headlines ripped from the *Conshohocken Recorder* from over the years include:

### 1886

"Chief of Police Hollands Arrested a Cow." The cow belonged to William Hallowell and was arrested for running the streets at large.

### 1910

"Officer Shoots at Escaping Prisoner." Michael Kennedy escaped Officer Heald as he was about to be placed in a cell; the officer shot at fleeing man, who made his escape.

### 1910

"Speak Easy Keeper Held for Trial." George E. Culp was held for $800 bail. Many witnesses testified to purchasing beer on Sunday at Culp's home on West Sixth Avenue near Whiskey Lane (today's Sutcliffe Lane).

### 1912

"Police Raid Crap Shooters." A fight among street gamblers at Seventh Avenue and Forrest Street brought the police, but crapshooters made their escape.

### 1912

"Gun Duel in Street Between Italians." Another victim of the lawless element of foreigners who were permitted to openly violate the law by carrying concealed deadly weapons. The two men got into a gun battle after drinking at a local tavern.

### 1913

"Police Shoot and Kill Man Charged with a Felony as He Was Escaping." Officers Ruth and Mason captured a man charged with a felony. The prisoner escaped and swam a creek, did not heed shots in air and police fired on him, inflicting fatal injuries.

### 1918

"Whole Police Force Offer Resignations." Men were dissatisfied with wages of eighty dollars per month for continuous work, would stay if paid ninety dollars.

# The Uniforms: Police, Firemen and Military

**1920**

"Policeman Tussles with a Bull." Officer Campbell made the most exciting arrest of his career when he arrested a bull. The bull escaped from his stable off North Lane and wandered into town, stepping on flowers on Fourth and Fifth Avenues.

**1925**

"Officer Jacquot Rounds Up Bad Gang." Officer Jacquot captured five youths who committed a series of robberies in different sections of the borough.

**1926**

"Hotel Keeper Under Bail, Caught with 5 Quarts of Moonshine." Officer Jacquot captured the proprietor of a hotel located at the corner of Elm and Poplar Streets with a bag containing five quarts of moonshine. When he was being put into the jail cell, he attempted to bribe Officers Jacquot, Donovan and Himes with fifty dollars, but his offer was refused.

**1927**

"Policeman Shot in Leg When Pistol Falls from Holster." Officer Donovan was wounded by accidental discharge of pistol in police station. The bullet just missed the chief. The bullet struck the officer in the left leg just above the ankle, took an upward course, passed out a short distance below the knee and embedded itself close to the top of the door leading to the corridor of the cell room, a few feet from where Chief William Heald was sitting.

**1928**

"Three More Dogs Shot Yesterday." In 1928, many *Recorder* articles reported packs of wild dogs roaming the streets of the borough.

**1928**

"Wounded Dog Bites Policeman." Officer Bosca was bitten on the hand three times after he shot a dog and tried to remove it from a house.

**1930**

"Police Raid Two Homes; Arrest Two." Armed with search warrants, Constable John Smith of West Conshohocken and Chief Donovan and Officers Williams and Bosco swooped down on two alleged bootleg establishments and seized á quantity of wine and beer. No frequenters were found in either place.

**1930**

"Council Takes Official Note of Brave Act." Commends Officer Harry Williams for recovering safe with $900. Alone, he chased fleeing bandits and exchanged shots. The two bandits broke into Almar Store located at Eighth Avenue and Hallowell Street.

**1930**

"Police Raid McGuire Place; Seize Liquor." Find Patrons in place and no one in attendance; a warrant was issued for Thomas McGuire, who escaped raiders.

**1936**

"Police Stop Craps Game." Raid place at 37 Fayette Street after orders to close were ignored. The raid was staged by Chief of Police Francis Blake and Officers Snear and Phillips. Less than two dollars was confiscated.

**1936**

"Policeman Kirkpatrick Shot in Hand by Constable in Party Watching for Suspect." Conshohocken police officer Ezekiel Kirkpatrick had his third and fourth fingers amputated following a shotgun blast that hit him in the hand at close range.

**1936**

"Police Riddle Bandits' Car with Bullets after Robbery; Recover Loot; Gang Escapes." Bandits broke into the tobacco warehouse of Stanley Szmigle on Elm Street. Police found bandits in car loaded with loot. The bandits were covered by policemen's guns, and the driver backed the car out and police started chase. The police fired nine shots into car, but bandits got away. Officer Walter Phipps was struck in the foot by return fire, but a steel beam saved his life.

**1944**

"Police Department Without Car for 53 Days." The police car smashed into the back of a fire truck when returning from a field fire at Tenth and Freedly Streets. Three officers had their own cars to drive, but the other three officers had to respond to borough calls on foot.

**1953**

"Officer Zadroga Ties a Runaway Horse to a Fire Hydrant after Merry Chase this Morning." Jesse Zadroga tied a horse to a fire hydrant outside the police station located at Hector and Harry Streets until rightful owner could be found.

## 1953

"Officer's Ankle Is Broken in Fight at Game." Officer Matt Doughtery had his ankle broken during a Thanksgiving day football game when he attempted to break up a fight at the A Field.

## 1957

"Officer Mazur Fires in Air, Two Men Halt." Officer Mazur heard the sound of breaking glass and saw four men running from the Washington Fire Company and ordered them to stop. When they didn't, Officer Mazur fired into the air, ordering them to halt. When he fired the shots, two of the men stopped and the other two got away.

## 1958

"5 Flee Store, Area Police Aid Capture." Conshohocken Police aided the Phoenixville Police by setting up a roadblock on Elm Street, helping to capture five men who robbed a Phoenixville furniture store.

## 1963

"Police Nab Six More in Gang Rumble." A total of sixteen young men had been arrested up to that point for participating in a "Gang Rumble." Officer George Bland responded to the fight at Elm and Poplar Streets. Bland ordered two youths to pull their car over, and the driver sped off. Officer Bland fired a shot at the fleeing car in the Connaughtown section. Officer Adam Pagliaro helped in the arrest in the Mogeetown section of Plymouth Township.

Michael Orler, the chief of police for the borough of Conshohocken in 2010, stated that in 2010, there are twenty full-time police officers and six police vehicles. The current budget for the year 2010 is $2.2 million, compared to just $2,500 in 1895. And when past headlines were brought to Chief Orler's attention, he stated that no gambling halls have been raided in recent years, nor have the police had to run down any bulls or horses running loose about the borough.

Conshohocken police officers can no longer discharge their guns into the air followed by a command to "HALT." Officers appointed to the police position in the early years did not receive any police training at all. By today's standards, potential police officer candidates must complete the ACT 12

Several of today's (2010) police officers line up in front of Borough Hall for a group photograph, including Conshohocken chief of police Michael Orler, standing in the back row second from left. In 1895, the annual police budget was $2,500; today's budget is $2.2 million. Conshohocken has twenty full-time officers and several part-time officers. *Courtesy of the Conshohocken Police Deparment.*

Police Training program before being considered for a police position. And one final thing: in the borough's 140-year police history, nowhere was there mentioned a female police officer. However, several years ago, Conshohocken hired its one and only female police officer, Connie Shaffer, who after working in Conshohocken is currently a police officer in Upper Merion Township. According to Orler, Conshohocken is ready and open to hire any female officer who qualifies for the police position.

A few of the police officers who have served the borough over the past decade include John Ellam, Tony Santoro, George Metz, John Storti, Matt Messenger, Andrew Carlin, Dave Zinni, James Carbo, Dave Lemon, Mike Kelly, Carmen Gambone, Dave Phillips, Shane Murray, Mike Connor and Jonathan Palmer.

## Eugene "Chick" Lucas, Lost in Action

It was a hot summer night in Conshohocken. On the evening of August 13, 1917, it was near closing time for most of the merchants along Fayette Street. Billy McGovern's cigar store located at 66 Fayette Street had a couple of locals still hanging around outside the store, as did Bob Crawford's cigar store, located for many years at Second Avenue and Fayette Street. On the corner of Hector and Ash Streets, Campbell's Furniture still had a potential customer or two milling about the store, and Little's Opera House was showing one of the many silent movies of the era at the movie house located on the second floor of its building at First Avenue and Fayette Street. The J.L. Oyster House at 48 Fayette Street always had a smell that would draw in hungry residents from the entire lower end of town, but nothing smelled sweeter than the warm aroma of Laise's Bakery on the corner of Elm and Fayette Streets.

Minutes before 8:30 on that Monday night, gunshots were heard coming from the corner of Elm and Fayette Streets. The sound of the shots pierced the heavy summer air and brought a community to its knees. Minutes later, Conshohocken police officer Eugene "Chick" Lucas staggered out of the Citron Building, turned right and headed up Fayette Street. When he reached Hector Street, several residents standing in front of Hart's cigar store noticed he was injured and assisted him to Dr. Fordyce's office located at Hector and Harry Streets. Once inside the office, Lucas collapsed and was declared dead at the doctor's office from a gunshot wound that ruptured the carotid artery in his neck.

Chick Lucas was a Conshohocken resident who was a former professional boxer, wrestler and race walker and, by all accounts of the day, was a very jovial individual. He was a very successful businessman and ran a paper-hanging and decorating business out of his storefront at 10 East Hector Street.

It was common practice in the early part of the last century to hire athletes or former soldiers to fill the position of police and law enforcement officers, and Chick was a perfect candidate. Conshohocken had four policemen in 1917, and when one of the full-time police officers was unable to work for a period of time, a special officer was hired to fill in. Officer George Ruth was on vacation, and Constable Ruggiero of Conshohocken swore in Lucas to fill in for Ruth.

On Chick's first day filling in for Ruth, Constable Ruggiero handed him a warrant filed by Madeline Nolen charging her husband, Michael Antolini—alias Black Mike, alias Mike Nolen, alias Mike Ralph, though we'll call him Black Mike—with desertion and abuse with intent to kill. Chick's second day on the job, he and Officer Clifford Campbell entered the Citron Building located on the corner of Elm and Fayette Streets, the home of Black Mike, to serve the warrant. The two officers traveled up three flights of blackened stairways to gain entry into Black Mike's apartment. The chain of events that followed started a twenty-year, headline-grabbing tale that ended on May 13, 1937.

When the officers reached Mike's apartment, the door was open and Black Mike was eating supper. Chick walked into the room with his club drawn and yelled, "Hands up." Black Mike responded by grabbing his revolver and fired three shots, one of them striking Chick above the collarbone. The bullet severed the carotid artery, and Chick fell to the floor. His partner, Campbell, also hit the floor to avoid being struck.

Black Mike escaped from the police and went on the run for five years until he was captured on October 30, 1922, in Uniontown, Pennsylvania, under the name of Joe Ross. Black Mike continued grabbing the headlines of local newspapers when on December 3, 1925, he and another convict escaped the Norristown prison by climbing over a wall. In April 1937, Black Mike filed a petition from Graterford Prison seeking a pardon while serving a fifteen- to seventeen-year prison term on a plea of guilty to second-degree murder. While waiting for a pardon, Black Mike died in Eastern State Penitentiary on May 13, 1937.

The name of Eugene J. "Chick" Lucas will live on in Conshohocken, Montgomery County and throughout the country. On May 19, 1995, the Montgomery County Police Officers Memorial was dedicated on the lawn of the Montgomery County Courthouse. The Conshohocken Police Department was well represented. In honor of Chick, his name is inscribed on the black granite memorial. Chick's name can also be found at Judicial Square in Washington, D.C., on the National Police Memorial.

According to current Conshohocken chief of police Mike Orler, a Police Star will be placed in the sidewalk outside of the former Citron Building with Chick's name inscribed.

# WASHINGTON FIRE COMPANY

## *It All Started in Stemple's Hall*

James Harry's drugstore was doing a thriving business on Fayette Street, as was James Wrigley, who sold boots and shoes. DeHaven & Brothers, Fulton & Company and Joseph Hampson all had solid businesses on the lower end of the town. Dozens of family-owned businesses were threatened in 1871 when a fire broke out at 72 Fayette Street, a general grocery store owned and operated by Mr. Morris.

It was a happy occasion on July 4, 1953, when this photograph was taken. Just before the annual Fourth of July parade, members of the Washington Fire Company posed for this picture on the old 1929 Metropolitan Pumper Truck. The three firemen are Lou Hale, John Ostapowicz and Warren Rinker sitting on the fender. *Standing up on truck, from left*: Jesse Stemple Jr., Jesse Stemple III sitting on Ted Lesinski's lap, Sam Januzelli, Carl Hylinski, Jerry Tancini and Bob Haines.

Ulysses S. Grant was president of the United States and the borough of Conshohocken was in its infancy, having been incorporated just twenty-one years earlier. The newly formed borough had no firefighting equipment, and a plea was sent to Norristown, some four miles from Conshohocken, for fire apparatus and volunteers. Norristown responded, and a message was sent to the Reading Railroad Station that Norris Fire Company was responding with its Pat Lyons Hand Engine. Members of the Norris Fire Company hustled along Ridge Pike pulling and pushing the Pat Lyons on foot. More than fifty volunteers from Norristown took turns running with the fire wagon into Conshohocken and sent a message to the onlookers: Conshohocken needed a fire company. A year later, a fire at the Plymouth Blast Furnace threatened the livelihood of dozens of residents, and the leading members of the town took action.

It was a cold Saturday evening on December 13, 1873, when thirty-eight residents gathered in Stemple's Hall on Forrest Street, just below Hector, for the purpose of organizing a hose and steam fire engine company. A temporary fire company was authorized, and Jacob M. Ulrick was selected as president of the company. James Colen was vice-president, John S. Moore was secretary and William Heywood was treasurer. A committee was also formed at this meeting to appoint a committee to secure a charter and charged each member a one-dollar fee for the purpose of purchasing a fire wagon.

The following week on December 20, 1873, members of this new hose and steam fire engine company selected a name for their company. As was the custom back then, a number of names were dropped into a hat, including Lincoln, Jefferson, Conshohocken, Washington and a few others. While it was not recorded who pulled the name, the slip of paper with "Washington" written on it was drawn, and as of December 20, 1873, a few months before the fire company was chartered, the name of the fire company was the Washington Hose and Steam Fire Engine Company No. 1.

## A Little Firehouse History

After using the barn of George Washington Jacoby for a couple of years to store its fire apparatus, the fire company purchased ground to build a two-story firehouse on West Hector Street. A two-story building, twenty-five by fifty feet, would cost $3,202. Members wanted a three-story facility but could not afford the additional $600. The company officials negotiated a low price with a promise to provide labor from its members.

Reuben Stemple was a hotelman and building contractor who landed the masonry and brick work for the erection of the Washington Fire Company's firehouse. In an effort to keep expenses low, the members of the company, following a hard day's work at the mills, raced to the firehouse to contribute to the lifting and moving of the cement, bricks, mixing motor and any other labor that was required. None of the firemen was paid, but as luck would have it, Reuben Stemple's hotel was just around the corner at 46 Fayette Street, and all of the workers often became very thirsty. Stemple would often send for a round of beer from the hotel by ordering the round written on a brick signed by Stemple. The bartender at the hotel would recognize Stemple's signature, pour a full round of beer for the thirsty workers and stack the bricks behind the bar.

Well, it didn't take long for the firemen-workmen to figure out a way to help themselves to a free party or two on Stemple. It became a frequent scene in the hotel bar that a rather large contingent of the firemen-workmen would enter the bar and start an argument with the barkeeper. While the barkeep engaged in a verbal tussle with the men, a few of the firemen would slip over and retrieve a few of the bricks with the coveted chalk markings that read "good for a few beers, R.S." Before long, the workmen had their own stash of bricks that proved as good as any credit card given in a bar today.

For what it's worth, it was reported that no firemen-workmen ever became intoxicated during the construction of the building.

Having celebrated more than 136 years of service and still growing, the rest, as they say, is Washington Fire Company history.

## A Few Fires for the Record

February 3, 1873: "John Wood & Brothers Explosion"
Considered the greatest catastrophe ever suffered by the borough of Conshohocken, a steam boiler exploded at 4:20 p.m. The tank went through the wall and flew across the canal and through the wall of another factory. Hunks of metal and shrapnel penetrated residents' walls and windows along Elm Street. The death toll would eventually rise to sixteen, with dozens more injured.

August 21, 1875: "Fire Totally Destroys Albion Print Works"
Washington Fire Company chief Frank Beaver nearly lost his life in the burning building caused by an exploding pressure tank.

June 10, 1879: "Fire at S&J Lees Nearly Destroys Entire Plant"
Daniel Foley, a Washington firefighter, was injured when he fell from a ladder while fighting the fire. Foley's unconscious body was carried back to the hotel he owned along the canal, and a physician determined that no broken bones could be found. Firemen worked for more than six hours to extinguish the blaze.

September 8, 1898: "The Conshohocken Brewery on Fire"
The Conshohocken Brewery, later the Gulph Brewery, was reported on fire by Mrs. B. DeHaven, who lived across the creek from the brewery. The tragedy at this fire was that the main building containing all the beer in storage was destroyed, and if that wasn't bad enough, all the beer in the process of being completed was also destroyed. On the upside the firemen had never before worked so hard to save a building. It was perhaps this fire that caused the formation of the George Clay Fire Company a year later.

September 10, 1917: "Explosion of Gas Rocks Whole Town"
Conshohocken and surrounding vicinities were rocked on a quiet Sunday morning when a ten-thousand-cubic-foot gas bag filled to capacity at the plant of the Process Oils Company, formerly the Henderson Supplee & Son flour and feed mill located on the berm bank, exploded with terrific force, leveling the building, shattering glass windows in buildings and homes for a distance of more than half a mile and rocking houses off their foundations. Borough officials called it a miracle when the three workers at the plant escaped injury.

June 1, 1920: "Moose Home Badly Damaged by Fire"
The headline for this fire was rather insignificant, as was the fire itself. However, Washington firefighter Miles Stemple was on the third floor of the Moose home, located at First Avenue and Harry Street, when the flooring gave way and Miles fell to the floor below. An injury to his arm was attended to, but Stemple said nothing about his internal injuries that damaged his liver. Miles Stemple, one of the first members of the fire company, died ten months later on August 20, 1921, due to injuries from the fall.

Miles responded to his final fire alarm on March 14, 1921, at the age of seventy-two years old. He is the only Conshohocken fireman to die in the line of duty.

May 22, 1923: "Early Morning Fire Destroys Harry St. School Building"
Mrs. George Westwood of East Third Avenue reported a fire at the Harry Street school that caused more than $60,000 in damage. Schoolchildren were given off until September. Both Conshohocken fire companies fought the overwhelming blaze and called in surrounding fire companies for assistance.

January 18, 1927: "Fire Destroys F.W. Woolworth's Building"
Firemen battled a blaze at the Woolworth's building on Fayette Street for more than seven hours and managed to save all adjoining businesses on the block. Residents from four apartments above the Woolworth's Store had to be rescued and taken out in nightclothes into the blinding snowstorm. Nearly a dozen firemen were injured at the scene, including George Wright of the Spring Mill Fire Company; Walter Pope of the Washington Fire Company; William Dewees, a seventy-year-old Washies firefighter; Edward McGuire of the George Clay Fire Company; and many more.

# The Uniforms: Police, Firemen and Military

January 28, 1928: "Washies Assist at Villanova College Fire"

With more than a foot of freshly fallen snow on the ground, the Washington Fire Company rushed to Villanova College to assist twenty-four other fire companies in extinguishing a blaze that threatened to burn the entire campus to the ground. (Keep in mind that Villanova consisted of three buildings in 1928.)

Dozens of firefighters were injured, including Washies assistant chief Johnny Riggs, who fell through a skylight into the burning building. Two other Washies firefighters were among dozens who had their hands frozen to the nozzles of the hoses that they were holding.

December 6, 1929: "McFadden's Feed Store Burns to the Ground"

George McFadden's feed store located on Elm Street near Poplar Street burned to the ground. The issue for Conshohocken's two fire companies was saving the entire row of houses as sparks landed on adjoining buildings throughout the blaze. Vincent Bonkoski, a member of the Conshohocken football team, reported the blaze. Clarence Strychirz, a twenty-one-year-old employee, risked injury when he saved the company truck. Unfortunately, there were no goods left to haul.

October 2, 1936: "Campbell's Furniture Store Destroyed by Fire"

The worst fire in the business section in the history of the borough totally destroyed the four-story store, dwelling, warehouse and garage of the Campbell Furniture Company at Hector and Ash Streets. The fire damaged more than a dozen buildings and caused about twenty-five families to flee from their homes in a driving rain. Patrolman Kirkpatrick discovered the early morning fire and aroused neighbors with revolver shots.

January 31, 1938: "25 Residents Escaped Fire at St. Mary's Home for Aged"

Twenty-five residents were forced to flee in nightclothes from an early Sunday morning fire at the St. Mary's Home for the elderly in West Conshohocken. The structure was formerly the home of George Bullock before becoming St. Mary's Orphanage and, later, St. Mary's Home for the Aged. Chief Herman Adams of the George Clay Fire Company stated that it was the worst fire in fifteen years and perhaps the worst nonindustrial fire in the borough's history. Washington Fire Company firefighter Johnny Riggs was overcome with smoke and was later treated.

December 27, 1956: "$400,000 Fire Wrecks Ancient Mill Property"

Four small industries housed in the Jim Hall Mill on River Road in West Conshohocken were gutted by an overnight fire. The explosion of six acetylene and oxygen tanks in two of the industries fed the flames. Companies responding included George Clay Washington Fire Company, Conshohocken Fire Company No. 2, Gladwyn, Bryn Mawr, Swedeland and the second alarmers of Willow Grove.

January 27, 1971: "Explosion on Front Street"

A cracked gas pipe on Front Street in West Conshohocken led to an explosion that shot flames more than one hundred feet into the air. Without a doubt, this was and will be remembered as West Conshohocken's worst disaster.

The explosion occurred at 9:45 p.m. on January 27, 1971, and when the ambulances finished carrying the bodies to four different hospitals by early the next morning, the worst had happened. Joseph Powers, nineteen, of 521 Ford Street and a George Clay firefighter, was killed; his twin brother, James, was treated for injuries and released. Four other residents of Front Street were also pronounced dead: Calvin Rupp, Michael Pruitt, Michele Pruitt and William Blair. Twelve houses were leveled, and the four hospitals combined reported that sixteen people were admitted, and thirty-five people were treated and later released.

May 10, 2005: "First Baptist Church Destroyed by Fire"

A fire at the First Baptist Church turned into a multi-alarm blaze when seven fire companies responded as the flames shot high into the air on a bright, sunny spring day in May 2005. Sparks from a contractor's torch accidentally started the blaze that eventually leveled the church. With the community's help, Reverend Brad Lacey reported that the church was being rebuilt as of 2010, with the outside completed and the interior expected to be completed in the near future.

August 13, 2008: "Fire of the Millennium"

It was the fire that no firefighter wanted to fight. On Wednesday, August 13, 2008, a fire later ruled accidental broke out at the construction site of the Millennium Stables. The fire quickly spread to two occupied buildings in the Riverwalk at the Millennium complex, forcing more than 300 firefighters to work through the night to bring the fire under control more than seven hours after it started. The fire affected 375 residents in 150 units; 1 firefighter was treated for injuries.

# NEW CENTURY, NEW FIRE COMPANY

### *Early in the Century*

By 1900, the town's population had swelled due to more mills operating within the borough. The new population forced residents to build family dwellings up the hill and on the side avenues. Conshohocken's population swelled so fast that by 1908, many of the immigrants were sleeping in tents throughout the borough on vacant lots. Town council considered building tent cities until the construction of new homes could catch up to the population. One *Conshohocken Recorder* headline declared, "The Town Has Run Out of Houses."

A series of fires in the upper end of town brought a group of citizens together to discuss a second fire company for Conshohocken. The Washington Fire Company, when formed in 1873, built its firehouse in what was the center of town at that time. However, as time passed, the town expanded, forcing the Washington Fire Company to do the impossible. The

When the Conshohocken Fire Company No. 2 was formed, it operated out of a garage at Toner's Hotel, located at Seventh Avenue and Maple Street. By early 1904, it had moved to the east side of town and responded to fire calls from a garage at Ninth Avenue and Harry Street. Three members of the No. 2 Company show off their horse-drawn water carriage.

early fire water wagons were all hand pulled and pushed. The weight of the wagon when filled with water made it nearly impossible to respond to a fire call up the steep grade of Fayette Street if it had rained or snowed. Keep in mind that Fayette Street was a dirt road back then, and rain made the street inches deep with mud for several days until the dirt would dry out. And we all know that when it snowed, of course there were no snowplows, making any trip up the hill impossible for the firemen.

In the fall of 1902, sixteen interested citizens gathered in the cigar store of Irving Nuss, located on West Sixth Avenue. The group of men determined that the borough residents needed a second fire company to work with the Washington Fire Company in an effort to keep the borough residents safe. Company meetings were later moved to Toner's Hotel, located at Seventh Avenue and Maple Streets. The men acquired a small hand-drawn hose carriage and operated from Toner's Hotel. In January 1903, the group filed for a charter, and on April 27, 1903, the State of Pennsylvania granted the charter. From that day on, the company was recognized as Conshohocken Fire Company No. 2.

## A Little Bit of Growth

Within a year, the company had moved to a garage on the corner of Ninth Avenue and Harry Street and, by 1906, had rebuilt the garage and replaced the small wagon with a chemical wagon. Conshohocken Fire Company No. 2 was known as the quiet fire company around town for more than a century. The Washington Fire Company always seemed to grab the headlines for fighting fires, marching in parades or just throwing one or more of its famous block parties. But in 1907, Company No. 2 became number one in grabbing headlines, hosting a parade and throwing a major block party.

In the fall of 1907, the No. 2 Fire Company's new chemical engine arrived in Conshohocken at a cost of $2,700. No. 2 Fire Company decided to show the rest of the county how to celebrate with a "housing" party. Invitations were sent out to every fire company in eastern Pennsylvania. Charles Parker was chairman of the event, with help from Harvey Shaw, Hugh Blair, Harry Logan, Louis O'Brien and Edward Grimshaw, just to name a few.

Officials mounted on horses led the parade, followed by members of town council and many county officials. The Washington Fire Company led the parade with apparatus drawn by ten horses. Eighty members of the company marched, and they were hosted by the Allentown thirty-five-piece band. Other bands included Philadelphia Drum Corps, Independent Drum

Corps, East Greenville Band, Spring City Band, Columbia Drum Corps, Merion Square Band and Spring Mill Band. Dozens of fire companies and more than one thousand firemen attended. Included was J. Elwood Lee Company's Auto Truck, decorated and filled with children.

Talk about a parade route where every house and building was decorated! The parade formed at East and West Sixth Avenue and moved on to Fayette Street, Fayette to Eleventh Avenue, counter marched to Hector Street, to Oak, to Elm, to Fayette, to Hector, to Poplar, to Elm, to Cherry, to Hector, to Jones, to Spring Mill Avenue, to Fourth Avenue, to Harry Street, to Sixth Avenue, to Maple, to Seventh, to Hallowell, to Eighth, to Harry, to Ninth Avenue, to Fayette and finally to the firehouse.

The Human Fire Company of Norristown was given the honor of housing the new apparatus. Parties were thrown at both the Washington Fire Company (you knew there was a party in it for Washies somewhere) and No. 2 Fire Company before, during and after the parade, and No. 2 hosted a major banquet in the evening hours in honor of the event.

Conshohocken Fire Company No. 2 never stopped growing, as it continued to purchase top-of-the-line equipment. It didn't hurt that in the early years, fire company officials worked with E.J. Wendell, and Charles Young, co-founders of the Hale Fire Pump Company. No. 2 has a long history with Hale Products.

In 1943, the No. 2 purchased the Uptown Social Club building, a one-story building adjoining the firehouse at Ninth Avenue and Harry Street. This allowed company officials to expand the firehouse. In 1947, the company purchased the property of John Hamilton at 819 Fayette Street for the purpose of erecting a handsome new firehouse with the main entrance on Fayette Street.

## But It's All About Today

For reasons unknown, the fire company never built its headquarters at 819 Fayette Street, but more than fifty-five years later, the company again purchased a Fayette Street property. In 2003, ribbon-cutting ceremonies were held for the new firehouse. In 2010, Conshohocken Fire Company No. 2 set a new standard in firefighting when the membership elected Jackie Pierce as the first female president of a fire company in the borough. Pierce had been an active firefighter in the company for many years before being elevated to president.

Future firemen and firewomen take a break at the Conshohocken Fire Company No. 2 in 1999. Today, a few of these youngsters are firemen at No. 2. *Seated, from left*: Brandon Mungon, Amy Costello, Rachel Hoagan, Danny Costello, Nicki Hogan, Matthew Costello, Elizabeth Costello and Mark Costello.

# CONSHOHOCKEN MILITARY

## *It Was a Civil War*

When John Brown raided Harpers Ferry in 1859, history states that he set in motion events that led directly to the outbreak of the Civil War in 1861. While the war might have begun in South Carolina on April 12, 1861, the widespread effects of the war reached clear across the country, into Conshohocken and beyond.

Men from the Conshohocken community and surrounding areas joined the war effort and served in the Pennsylvania Eighty-eighth Division, Company C, out of the Spring Mill section of Conshohocken. Before the war ended in 1865, a total of 200,000 Americans were killed in action and a total of more than 600,000 Americans lay dead from war-related wounds and disease.

Dr. David Richardson Beaver served Conshohocken as the town physician for fifty-nine years before passing away in 1923. Dr. Beaver served as an assistant surgeon in the Civil War from April 13, 1864, until June 11, 1864, in the Pennsylvania volunteers and also as a first assistant surgeon of the 191st Regiment. Beaver served with Grant's army until the capture of Lee, after which he was ordered to Harrisburg and mustered out of service in July 1865. Dr. Beaver served in the Battles of the Wilderness, Laurel Hill, Bethesda Church, Spotsylvania Court House, North Anna, Cold Harbor, Peebles Farm, Weldon Railroad and Petersburg.

In 1870, Dr. Beaver came to Conshohocken as an assistant to Dr. John K. Read and purchased a house at 405 Fayette Street, where he lived until his death. He later set up his office next door at 401 Fayette Street, currently the site of the 401 Diner. His daughter Margaret and son-in-law Stuart Maloney later moved into his house and lived there until the late 1940s.

Ebenezer Lancaster was a Conshohocken native and a member of Company E of the Fifteenth Pennsylvania Cavalry. He enlisted on August 22, 1862, and died in Nashville, Tennessee, a year later. John Pugh was a lifelong resident of the borough who served several years during the war. Pugh later became the president of Conshohocken's First National Bank and owner of the S&J Pugh Feed Business once located at the foot of the Matsonford Bridge.

Thomas H. Ramsey lived most of his life in the Spring Mill section of Conshohocken, and when the Civil War broke out, Ramsey answered President Lincoln's first call for volunteers. He enlisted in the 138th Regiment Pennsylvania and served through the entire war. He was in the campaign in the Wilderness and was wounded at Chancellorsville. He was also in numerous battles and marched with Sherman to the sea.

John Baker posted a brilliant war record. He was captured at the Battle of Chancellorsville and returned to Conshohocken, taking part in the hotel business for many years following the war. Jonathan Rogers and William McFeeters, both members of the 88th Pennsylvania Volunteers and lifelong residents of the borough, played a part in Conshohocken's effort in the war. John J. Murphy was a member of Company G, 114th Regiment, and served three full years, fighting in the Battles of Fredericksburg, Chambersburg and Gettysburg. James Palmer, George W. Keys, George Pitman, John Bemesderfer, Robert Herron, Nathan Jones and Jonathan Rogers were a few of the dozens of Conshohocken residents who lived and worked in the borough before, during or after the Civil War. Three Conshohocken volunteers were killed in action, fifteen were wounded and two were taken prisoners of war and released.

## World War I: They Were Proud, but Not So Few

The borough of Conshohocken holds a very unique designation that no other community in America can claim title to. During World War I, the borough of Conshohocken sent more men and women off to serve in the United States military than any other community in America per capita. Robert Bell, Louis Bickings, Harry Dembowski, Daniel Donovan, Francis DeMario, Harry Wertz, John Wood, Samuel Gordon Smyth, Frank Hitner, George Hastings, James Koch and George Rodenbaugh were among the hundreds of Conshohocken residents who went off to war between 1916 and 1918.

Shortly after the signing of the Armistice at Complegne, France, that brought a close to World War I on November 11, 1918, the United States Congress recognized Conshohocken's efforts during the war. A merchant marine ship was named the *Conshohocken* in honor of the town's war service. The SS *Conshohocken* was launched on January 31, 1920, from the Sun Ship Yard and was christened by Mrs. Geoffrey Creyke, wife of the assistant to the vice-president of the Emergency Fleet Corporation.

The SS *Conshohocken* was an eleven-thousand-ton cargo carrier and was the last of the series of ships built under the supervision of the Emergency Fleet Corporation and the twenty-third ship to be launched at the yards of the Sunbuilding Company in Chester, Pennsylvania.

## World War II: They Were Something Special

January 21, 1941, was a mild, sunny day as eighty-eight members of Battery C lined up outside their headquarters located at 918 Maple Street. The soldiers marched up Ninth Avenue to Fayette Street, and a parade led by Betty Colburn, a drum majorette, and the Conshohocken High School Band marched down Fayette Street toward the train station, with a crowd of thousands of residents and schoolchildren cheering them on.

Conshohocken's Battery C mustered into the Pennsylvania National Guard on October 28, 1940, more than a year before the United States became involved in World War II. Battery C of the 1st Howitzer Battalion of the 166th Artillery left the Conshohocken train station for Camp Shelby, Mississippi, and didn't return for five years.

The men spent two years in Mississippi and then went to Camp Blanding in Florida and later to Fort Gordon and finally to Fort Dix in New Jersey. Once the men of Battery C left the States, they headed to North Africa,

A few of the eighty-eight-member Battery C of Conshohocken pose for a group photograph at their headquarters, once located at 918 Maple Street, before marching off to war on January 21, 1941. Battery C mustered into the Pennsylvania National Guard on October 28, 1940. Battery C of the 1st Howitzer Battalion of the 166th Artillery left the Conshohocken train station for Camp Shelby, Mississippi, in 1941 and didn't return for five years.

crossed the Mediterranean Sea to Italy and then engaged in some of the worst fighting of the war. Battery C moved on to southern France, arriving on D-Day, August 15, 1944. The men later went on to Germany and Austria before the war finally ended.

Perhaps one of the highlights for the men of Battery C was their part in taking out the Bridge on the Rhine. Battery C was part of the 938th Field Artillery's C Battery and Company A of the 630th Tank Destroyers. After more than six hours of heavy fire, the bridge went down. The west span had been blown from its main support and was a twisted heap of steel littering the river below.

By July 1945, after fifty-six months, the final members of Battery C returned home; 12 members of the unit lost their lives during combat in Europe. It was reported in 1945 that 1 out of every 7 residents in the

In 2002, a few Conshohocken veterans from Veterans of Foreign Wars Post 1072 honored Conshohocken fallen heroes on Pearl Harbor Day at the borough's monument. *Standing, from left:* Joe Thomas, Gerald McTamney, Joe Graham and Joe Horn.

borough was serving in the armed forces. Conshohocken had more than 1,600 residents serving in 1944, including more than two dozen females. West Conshohocken reported that 1 in every 6 residents was serving in the war effort. In all, 32 Conshohocken residents lost their lives during World War II, and West Conshohocken sacrificed 10 residents.

The Conshohocken boroughs were well represented in all wars, including the Korean War, Vietnam and every war since. Our young soldiers fight and sacrifice with the same pride as our neighbors and relatives have since the Civil War.

Conshohocken's highest-ranking military official is General Anthony C. Zinni, a four-star retired general of the United States Marine Corps. Zinni grew up in the Connaughtown section of Conshohocken, is a Villanova University graduate and joined the Marine Corps in 1961. General Zinni's military service took him to over seventy countries before he retired in 2000.

Part Five

# A Little Education
# on Schools

## IT STARTED IMMEDIATELY

When Conshohocken was incorporated, one of the first concerns of the borough's new government was education. Less than two months after incorporation, on July 8, 1850, a school board was organized and consisted of the following members: John Wood, president; Benjamin Harry, treasurer; David L. Wood, secretary; and Frederick Naile, James Swenk and Hugh McCallum, board members.

A little red house built in the early 1830s located on West Elm Street next to the Presbyterian church was in use as a township schoolhouse. Once the borough incorporated, taking half the land from Plymouth Township and the other half from Whitemarsh Township, the schoolhouse formerly located in Plymouth Township was now within the boundaries of Conshohocken.

The school board quickly made it a borough school, where twenty-five pupils enrolled with one teacher. Mr. Karr served as the school principal. The student population quickly outgrew the little red schoolhouse, and the school board moved the student body to the old Temperance Hall, later the site of Harrold's Hotel, also located on West Elm Street. Mr. Boggs was principal in the Temperance Hall School.

A year later, the school board purchased land on Forrest Street below Hector Street and built a schoolhouse. This building later was purchased by Davey Stemple and became known as Stemple's Hall, where the Washington Fire Company was later organized. While at the school on Forrest Street, Mr. Schuick served as principal.

The 1969 class photograph of third-grade students from Hervey S. Walker Elementary School included *front row, left to right*: Nicholas Malantonio, Steven Bolger, Thomas Kennedy and Dennis Kelly. *Second row, left to right*: Marcia Intrieri, John Boccella, Joanne Suchecki, Michael Markoski and Chris Ingram. *Third row, left to right*: Donna Donovan, Pattie House, Frances Balkiewicz, Debbie Banks and Bridget Piatelli. *Back row, left to right*: Dorothy Murray, Debbie White, Darryl Lee, Matthew Wertz, Julie Ball, Michael Orler, Daniel Yucalevich, Susan Lontkowski, Renee Dean and Mary Wambold.

Within five years, the school board had used three different locations for the school building, and once again the schoolhouse became too small to accommodate the growing number of students. In 1855, the school board purchased another lot of ground from Theodore Trewendt for $900 to build a more suitable schoolhouse. The property was located high on a hill overlooking the turnpike (now the 100 block of Fayette Street), backing up to Forrest Street. On a resolution passed by the school board on July 24, 1855, a contract in the amount of $3,100 was awarded to the Hinds and Famous Construction Company to build a schoolhouse. The building was two stories high and contained four classrooms. It was built and ready for classes in November 1855.

Daniel Ermentrout was named principal of the grammar school, now containing about fifty pupils. He resigned in 1857 and was replaced by Jesse Hall. Hall remained as principal until 1864, when he resigned, and Reuben

F. Hoffecker was appointed principal. Hoffecker led the charge to build the public school at Third Avenue and Harry Street, a school that would eventually bear his name.

## Montgomery County Taps the Best

Reuben Hoffecker was a leading educator of the day, and when he accepted the job as school principal in 1864, the school was already overcrowded with more than 230 pupils. Within five years, Hoffecker convinced the school board to build a modern-day facility at Third Avenue and Harry Street. It was first named the Third Avenue Grammar School and later the Harry Street School.

Hoffecker organized the public schools of Conshohocken into a system that became more effective than any other school system in Montgomery County. Graduation of pupils was a new idea in education when Hoffecker introduced the ceremony in Conshohocken in 1872. Hoffecker also introduced graded courses and school libraries.

There was no doubt that Reuben Hoffecker was the pioneer educator of the borough of Conshohocken, and other school systems and school districts took notice. When Montgomery County created the post of county superintendent of schools, it tapped Conshohocken's own Reuben Hoffecker, who resigned from Conshohocken in 1878 to share his knowledge with the rest of the county.

Following Hoffecker as principal in Conshohocken was J.W. Schlichter, followed by J. Addison Jones, who served one year. Then John Harley served until 1892. Conshohocken then hired J. Horace Landis as principal, and he served until 1896, when he was elected superintendent of borough schools, being the first to hold that office in Conshohocken. In 1904, following a very successful twenty-five-year run as county superintendent of schools, Reuben Hoffecker resigned his post.

Once again, Montgomery County came calling upon Conshohocken, asking for Landis to fill Hoffecker's shoes at the county level of superintendent of schools. Landis resigned in Conshohocken in 1904 to do just that. As Montgomery County called on Conshohocken for school leadership, it acknowledged the borough's ability to recognize talented educators. Landis was an ardent advocate of consolidated schools and worked continuously to enact the legislation necessary for the establishment of such schools. When the legislature permitted the consolidation of township schools, Landis personally carried on a campaign of education among the school directors and parents, showing the advantages of consolidated schools, which would give all pupils the same educational advantages enjoyed by children of the larger towns.

Many of the programs enacted by Montgomery County superintendent of schools Reuben Hoffecker and J. Horace Landis were recognized and implemented at the state level. The county's first two superintendents were at the forefront of modern educational advances in the state of Pennsylvania, and it all started in Conshohocken.

On March 2, 1922, the Harry Street Grammar School was renamed the Reuben F. Hoffecker Grammar School in honor of Hoffecker, who had passed away in 1921.

## CATHOLICS, CONSHOHOCKEN WAS THE FIRST

St. Matthew's Roman Catholic Church was established in 1851 under the guidance of Reverend Patrick A. Nugent. Twelve years later, in 1863, Reverend Richard F. Kinahan recognized the need for a Catholic school teaching the religious values of the church. In September 1864, St. Matthew's School was established in the basement of the church, then located on the corner of Hector and Harry Streets. Three teachers—Mary Ella McCullough, Elizabeth O'Brien and Mary McGuire—established the teaching guidelines for the school. By June 1865, more than fifty students were attending the basement school.

By 1866, St. Matthew's School had established advanced courses, or high school education, which led to the school's first high school graduating class. One hundred years later, in 1966, when St. Matthew's High School (then located at 1300 Fayette Street) changed its name to Archbishop Kennedy High School in honor of Reverend Thomas F. Kennedy, it was the oldest Catholic high school in the United States.

By 1869, more than one hundred students attended the basement school, and Father Kinahan purchased property on Hector Street east of Ash Street for the purpose of building a schoolhouse for St. Matthew's pupils. Acting as the architect, and with no permits needed, Father Kinahan opened the new school in 1872 at a cost of $15,000. The new two-story structure consisted of ten classrooms and six cloakrooms. Nine of the classrooms were for elementary studies, and one classroom was used for high school studies. Keep in mind that not many students pursued a high school education; in 1895,

St. Matthew's Church established a school in the basement of its church in 1851. By 1872, the parish had purchased ground on East Hector Street and built a school. Bertha Knicht was one of seven graduating students from St. Matthew's School in 1895; she lived to be ninety-five years old and passed away in 1974.

only seven students graduated. Restrooms were later added in a separate building located behind the school, replacing the antiquated outhouses. The school was being used as an elementary school into the early 1970s.

In 1993, Archbishop Kennedy High School closed its doors and merged with Bishop Kenrick High School, renamed Kennedy-Kenrick High School, located in Norristown. In 2010, Kennedy-Kenrick closed its doors, leaving both Conshohocken and Norristown without a Catholic high school.

## SAY GOODBYE TO THE PUBLIC SCHOOL

Reuben Hoffecker established Conshohocken's first public high school, located next to the elementary school on East Third Avenue. The first high school graduating class was in 1872. Once again, the borough's population growth forced the expansion of school facilities, and in 1913, the borough school board purchased property on the corner of Seventh Avenue and Fayette Street. Two lots, 40 feet on the corner, were owned by Romandus Scheetz, and were purchased for $5,000. Four lots adjoining, owned by Mrs. William Maconachy, were purchased for $3,500, giving a total tract of land 120 by 187 feet.

The seven-classroom high school, complete with two drinking fountains and a chemistry laboratory, cost $50,000 when completed in 1913. In 1922, the first of several expansion projects was completed with the addition of a gymnasium and auditorium.

In the mid-1960s, many small steel towns in the state of Pennsylvania recorded a steady declining enrollment of high school students. Act 299, passed by the Pennsylvania state legislature, defined the required enrollment that school districts must meet in order to remain open and independent; this was not met by several local school districts, including Conshohocken.

On June 8, 1966, the ninety-fifth and final commencement exercises were held in the high school auditorium. In the fall of 1967, Conshohocken high school residents were required to report to Plymouth Whitemarsh High School located on Germantown Pike in Whitemarsh Township. The school operates under the subname of the Colonial School District.

The following is the first verse of the Conshohocken High School song, rendered for the last time at the 1966 graduation ceremony:

*Far above life's rushing waters,*
*Mingled with the blue*
*Stands our noble Alma Mater,*
*Glorious to view,*
*When life's trials dark assail us,*
*Firm and strong we stand*
*Hail to the dear Alma Mater,*
*Fairest in the land*

# CONSHOHOCKEN COMMUNITY COLLEGE

Talk of a community college in Montgomery County started in 1961. By 1963, a bill was introduced in the state legislature for the establishment of a community college. In August 1964, a steering committee delivered a plan to the State Board of Education, which gave the plan approval, and on December 8, 1964, the founding of the college was announced.

# A Little Education on Schools

The timing of Act 299, forcing the merger of Conshohocken High School and leaving a vacant school building in Conshohocken, was good for the newly formed Montgomery County Community College. The first classes of the new school met at the old Conshohocken High School on October 3, 1966.

The Montgomery County Community College, located at 612 Fayette Street, was the fourth such institution in the state of Pennsylvania. Governor William W. Scranton dedicated the facility. When it was opened, 440 full-time students and 150 evening students were attending the school at a yearly tuition rate of $975. Students at that time were only required to pay one-third of the cost, as the county and state paid the other two-thirds if needed.

The college was located in Conshohocken for five years and showed steady growth. In 1966, the school had 590 total students. In 1971, it had 3,300 full- and part-time students. The faculty expanded from 17 in 1966 to 90 in 1971, and the school required nine locations in the borough, including a church and former funeral parlor, to house the students for classes.

In January 1972, the four-building complex located on 186 acres in Blue Bell, Pennsylvania, was completed and ready for occupancy. Within ten years, the school more than doubled in population. In 2008, the college was ranked first in the nation for its use of technology by the Center for Digital Education. Today, it has more than thirty thousand alumni.

For Montgomery County Community College, it all started in Conshohocken back in 1966, thanks to Act 299.

Part Six

# Sports

## BASEBALL, THE FACT AND THE FUNNY

Chot Wood, Knute Lawler, Ira "Whitey" Mellor, Roy "Whitey" Ellam, Jack Harrold, Jack Gillespie, Perk Smith, Dave Traill, Paul Burton, Leo Redmond, Ray "Binkie" Fairlie, Sam Webster, Jim Kriebel, Bill Ford, John "Pud" Johnson, Ed Harrison, Jack Crimean, Bill "Parry" Murphy and Jack McDade were some of the best baseball players of an era ago to ever pick up a baseball in the borough of Conshohocken.

Young baseball stars of today start young and play in the Conshohocken Little League organization, a solid Little League program that has been in the borough since 1955. Back in the 1920s and throughout the 1930s, the borough had midget baseball leagues. Teams like the Greyhounds, Notre Dame Midgets, the Hollyhawk Aces and the Connaughtown Red Raiders would square off in open fields and later at Sutcliffe Park.

Baseball in the borough of Conshohocken dates back to the 1870s, before Major League baseball was organized. Baseball was the first branch of organized sports to be played here. One of the few flat fields in the borough was located on Washington Street along the canal, east of Cherry Street, later called "the Meadow." There was no infield or diamonds; rocks or other items were used as bases; catchers had no protective gear and no padded baseball gloves.

The first organized team recorded playing the sport was the Nerve of Conshohocken, made up of local steelworkers and young men. Andy Loughery and Johnny Heffelfinger pitched for the Nerve, and George Buck and Michael McCall were catchers. Other players included Jack Harold and Horace Cassey.

The Aerials followed the Nerve and carried several of the first team's players but added young talent like Dick Blake, Fred Wood, Edwin Harrison and Bill Davis. Then came the great teams of the late 1890s, and Conshohocken soon joined much more competitive leagues, like the Schuylkill Valley Baseball League and leagues in and around the city of Philadelphia. History notes that league meetings would often be held at McCall's cigar store on Hector Street or similar places in Norristown.

Conshohocken's glory years in the sport of baseball were many, but there was nothing like the 1920s, when the manufacturers of the borough formed a league with dozens of teams. Some companies had so many employees that they formed their own league within the company. In the John Wood Manufacturing Company, each department had a team. One write-up in the local paper told of the Alan Wood teams, the Puddlers and the Helpers, facing off. In a scoreless game in the fifth inning, the Puddlers scored twenty-five runs and the Helpers called off the remainder of the game. Both teams retired to the shade of the trees at the Ninth Avenue field and, with smiles on their faces, relaxed with cool, refreshing drinks—and we're not talking soda pop.

After-game refreshments didn't always go down so well; often the winners and losers would join together for postgame refreshments, as they did back in 1905. The Standard Athletic Club from West Philadelphia was on the losing end when the Conshohocken Athletic Association beat them late in the game 4–3. The losers decided to "do up the town," and a riot resulted. Conshohocken police officer William Heald walked into the middle of the fight, featuring brass knuckles and blackjacks, and was quickly pummeled. Many of the West Philly boys made their way to the train but had police officers waiting for them at the end of the line. Most of the visitors spent the night in jail.

By 1908, the Conshohocken burgess had had enough. Fred J. Bloomhall notified all organized baseball clubs that ball games on Sundays were no longer allowed to be played within the borough limits. Bloomhall gave notice that warrants would be issued and arrest would result in fines for each offender, calling them a "gang of half-grown Rowdys."

## Then Came the Girls

As early as 1910, traveling female baseball teams would visit Conshohocken to engage in ball games with local teams, often drawing several thousand spectators to the fields. In 1914, the Female Ball Tossers of Conshohocken played the visiting New York Bloomer Girls in a game played at the Meadow. While the New Yorkers won a close game 4–3, the local headlines declared that more than one thousand spectators witnessed the game, some walking for miles, but less than half paid money to view the game. The field was surrounded with a canvas enclosure, but hundreds of spectators stood on top of dozens of boxcars on the siding along the Reading Railroad to view the Bloomer Girls perform on the diamond.

In the 1920s, Bloomer Girl baseball teams became more popular when other small, local towns fielded competition. In 1922, the Swedeland Bloomer Girls visited Conshohocken for a game against the Lady Tigers. Conshohocken won the game 7–6 behind the fine play of Kate Davis, Mary Gillespie, Kriebel, Sedor and Smith.

By the 1930s, many of the Bloomer Girl teams were playing members of the opposite sex, sometimes resulting in an embarrassing situation. In 1933, the visiting Rold Gold Bloomer Girls from Tacony bested the boys of the Baptist church, 7–5. Betty Sell was the opposing pitcher who pitched five innings for the Bloomers and, in the sixth inning, threw out a Baptist runner at the plate from deep center field.

## The Funny

While Conshohocken baseball fielded some of the county's greatest players, as mentioned earlier, the town didn't always take the sport so seriously. A headline from August 8, 1941, in the *Conshohocken Recorder* says it all: "Trick Donkeys Make 'Donkeys' out of Local Men in Baseball Game." A paragraph from the article reads:

> *The score was Conshohocken Lions 3, Business Men 2, in the annual thrilling, spilling, milling, Burro Baseball Game staged under the auspices of the rip roarin Lions. An Audience that overflowed the grandstands and numbered dozens of standees howling with continual glee as the players hit, fell from balking donkeys, missed base by a donkey's nose, and engaged in all the novel athletics that a Burro Baseball Game affords. The game was held at the Conshohocken Athletic Field for charity.*

Another fun annual outing in the early part of the last century was the annual Thin Men versus the "Fattys." The Penn Club of Conshohocken for many years hosted the event that involved over-the-hill baseball players. The thin ballplayers were on one team, while residents who were, shall we say, a little beefy played for the other team. Over the years, members of the Penn Club would travel to different locations—always with a watering hole nearby. In 1913, according to the *Recorder*, Broad Axe was the site. The headline and part of the article read like this:

> *"Thin Men Defeat The 'Fattys' At Baseball. Penn Club Holds Last Outing of The Season at Broad Axe."*
>
> *"Has Beens" Show a Good Return To Form But The Fat Men Led Until The Heat Overcame Them.*
>
> *Straight as the crow flies journeyed the members of the Penn Club to that old historical place, called the Broad Axe. Built on the old Indian trail, that winds its way down to the hills and valleys, through which runs the Schuylkill River.*
>
> *The Broad Axe has a history of its own. The original Hotel was owned by a widow named Mrs Betty Hatchet. Known near and far for her beauty, wisdom ways, and especially for the quality of Ale.*

And that, my friend, is what made the two-hour journey to the ball field worth it: the quality of ale. The Thin Men were led by Captain William Little, who owned the opera house once located at First Avenue and Fayette Street, while the "Fattys" were led by Fred J. Broomhall, burgess of Conshohocken. Harrison, Jones, Tracy, Carroll and Bodey started for the Fat Men, while Siegler, McGrath, Ruth, Donnelly and Hellinger played well for the Thin Men. Following the 8–6 Thin Men victory, all would enjoy dinner at the Broad Axe, and following dinner, most of the members of the Penn Club would go to Willow Grove Park and enjoy music and dancing.

## Still Funny

The Washington Fire Company became one of the best firefighting units in the state of Pennsylvania, but back in the 1880s, it seems as though it was somewhat of an embarrassment to the community. The Washies decided to form a baseball team and travel to other towns, carrying the good name of Conshohocken with them to challenge other fire companies to nine innings.

In the early 1880s, our proud firemen traveled to Chester to take on members of the Franklin Fire Company. The Chester newspaper gave a great account of the game:

> *The Washington boys of Conshohocken put out a big fire with celerity, but they are not there so to speak when it comes to playing ball with the Franklin*

# Sports

*Fire laddies of Chester. By arrangement, nines from the two companies met at Houston Park yesterday afternoon in a friendly contest on the diamond, and before four innings were played it was painfully evident that the visitors would be very badly left.*

The Franklin nine posted 14 runs in the third inning and another 22 runs in the eighth inning and went on to win the contest 47–10, but that was not the embarrassing part. It seems as though the Washies' uniforms were clearly a sight to see, or as the Chester newspaper stated, "The suits of the visitors which were new and novel, were the most stunning ever seen on a ball field."

Jumbo Wagner, who covered first base for the Washies, wore a gray shirt that covered a bay window so large that he was unable to see whether his foot was resting on the canvas bag. One pant leg was of light blue chintz and the other of red calico, while his stockings were of a damask tint. He spliced together two belts to go all the way around him. Moconachy covered second base with patent leather pumps and himself with dust and glory. Earl, in right field, wore blue socks, with one leg of his knee breeches a navy blue and the other a Bismarck brown; he also wore a calico cap. The man behind the batter looked like a Bridgeport butterfly on dress parade, and it was believed at first that he was the missing Joseph of the coat of many colors.

While each and every player was described from head to foot, many funny incidents were played out during the game, including a foul ball off the bat that the catcher missed and the ball continued to travel, hitting the umpire in the vest pocket and setting fire to a box of matches. Of course, the Washies firefighters weren't so funny then, as they sprang into action to douse the flames and dust off the umpire before going back to taking a pounding on the field.

While Conshohocken had some great fun with the sport of baseball, it should never overshadow the fact that the borough has produced dozens of championship teams and hundreds of great baseball players.

## Football, Tough as Steel

The state of Pennsylvania is the home of professional football, and Conshohocken was certainly at the forefront of professional football in its infancy. In the fall of 1893, Conshohocken formed its first football team, sponsored by the Young Men's Athlete Association (YMAA), and was called

Ironmen. Conshohocken's first organized team played two years before the first all-professional game was played in Latrobe, Pennsylvania. Latrobe beat neighboring Jeannette 12–0. Each player was paid ten dollars for his services.

The Conshohocken Ironmen consisted of thirteen players, most of whom worked in the town's steel and iron mills—hence the name the Ironmen. The Ironmen played their games on the east side of Fayette Pike between Eighth and Ninth Avenues. Part of the property was later occupied by the O'Brien family and is currently the site of the Mason's Lodge.

Members of the first team included Sam Wright, Ben Cressman, Charles Herron, Fred and Arthur Clark (sons of Charles Heber Clark, nationally known author under the pen name of Max Adler), Eugene and Bud Beaver (sons of Dr. David Beaver, a Civil War surgeon with his home and office at the northeast corner of Fourth Avenue and Fayette Street, currently the Bank of America), Alan Caine, George Lukens (later Dr. Lukens) and Louis and Max Vielhaber.

Conshohocken joined the professional ranks of the sport in 1914 under the management of Robert J. Crawford, a cigar store owner and former Conshohocken athlete. The Conshohocken football teams from 1914 to 1922 became known as the "Golden Age of Football" in the borough. Conshohocken's 1919 team went undefeated and was recognized as the United States Eastern Seaboard Champions. The National Football Hall of Fame, located in Canton, Ohio, acknowledged Conshohocken's achievement and accepted the team photograph. It hangs on display on a rotating basis with other great teams of the era.

One side note to Conshohocken's professional era: in 1917, Jack Kelly was a running back and receiver for the Conshohocken pros. Kelly went on to become one of the most accomplished oarsmen in the history of the sport of rowing. He was later the father of Grace Kelly, actress and princess of Monaco.

Johnny "Jack" McBride, a Conshohocken native, went on to play with the very first New York Giants team in 1925. McBride—a Syracuse University All-American football player in 1924—played for the Giants for ten years. In 1925, he ran out of the backfield with the great Jim Thorpe, the former Canton Bulldogs standout. McBride was a shining star in the newly developed professional football league, and in 1927, he was named the league's Most Valuable Player over Harrold "Red" Grange. McBride never played a down of football at Conshohocken High School, where he attended, graduating in 1918. Conshohocken High School didn't have a football team until 1923.

Conshohocken enjoyed many great seasons on the football field during the 1920s, '30s and '40s, featuring many of the town's great athletes. Names like Bonkoski, Mellor, Webster, O'Donnell, Fox, Marine, Borzelleca, Cannon, Snear, Potteiger, Wood, Lawler, Campbell and Pettine would light up the newspaper headlines week after week. But of the hundreds of football teams fielded over more than one hundred years in the borough, no rivalry was greater than the twenty-three games played between St. Matthew's High School and Conshohocken High School.

It started in 1925, when Conshohocken High School beat St. Matthew's 40–6. Conshy High bested the Catholics again in 1926, 7–0. But St. Matthew's gained revenge in 1927 when, with three minutes remaining in the game, Lou Devaney found an opening from the five-yard line for the game's only score and a 7–0 victory for St. Matthew's. The two teams would not meet again until 1944, and a twenty-year Thanksgiving Day rivalry began.

Today's young residents could never understand the meaning of these games, when six to eight thousand residents would pack the Conshohocken A Field on Thanksgiving morning. Teams would report to the field at 8:00 a.m. for pregame drills. Parades from each school would form and march up Fayette Street, where every merchant posted signs in their windows rooting for one team or the other or, in some cases, for both schools. The parades would turn on Eleventh Avenue and on to the field with the school's marching band, followed by the cheerleaders and fans into the stadium. Ten of the twenty games played from 1944 to 1964 were decided by seven points or less.

Starting in 1944, St. Matthew's won five of the first six games played. The game they didn't win was a 0–0 tie in 1947. When the final game was played in 1964, St. Matthew's won 25–18, winning the series 10–7 with three ties. Never again will Conshohocken experience the rivalry of the Catholics versus the Publics, as both schools are no longer part of the borough.

# BASKETBALL, IT'S ABOUT THE HALL OF FAME

Even the biggest Conshohocken basketball fans won't remember seeing or hearing of some of the great basketball games being played by the Knights of Columbus. The Knights played their home games at the former Grand Army of the Republic Hall, located on the corner of West Third Avenue and Forrest Street, later a furniture warehouse and St. Coptic Church and currently an office building. Nor would those same fans recall any games being played at the old Presbyterian church once located on the corner of Elm and Maple Streets. Other early locations for the wire cage-playing field included the former Steen Livery Stable, later converted for Moser Glass Works on Hector Street near Poplar Street.

Many a basketball game was played at the original Washita Hall, part of William Little's opera house once located on the corner of First Avenue and Fayette Street, currently Light Parker Furniture Store. When the new Washita Hall opened on the corner of Sixth Avenue and Harry Street, the Church Basketball League played for years on the second floor. Many basketball games were also played on the second floor of the Knights of Columbus Hall when it was built in 1925. Nowadays, the building is the Great American Pub Restaurant and Bar. Since 1953, more basketball has been played in the borough at the Conshohocken Fellowship House than any other location in the history of the borough.

In 1895, Conshohocken formed a basketball team sponsored by the Pioneer Club of Conshohocken. The sport of basketball was still in its infancy, having been pioneered in Springfield, Massachusetts, in 1892. The rules were different and the court was different: nine players from each team were on the playing field, but only two players from each team were permitted to score.

High school basketball in the borough was very popular, with St. Matthew's and Conshohocken High Schools both fielding teams going back to the early part of the last century. The great players of both schools number in the hundreds, but for Conshohocken High School, a 63–48 victory on a snowy March night in the spring of 1964 over Coudersport gave Conshohocken its only high school state championship in the borough's history.

Head Coach Joe Kirby led his squad of players to the Class C State Championship. The list of players on that team included Joe Lewandowski, Francis Omar, John Reuben, Adam Ciccotti, Michael Ethridge, Michael DePalma, Robert Graham, Thomas "Buddy" White, Michael Howell, Joseph McFadden, Harry Kitt and Ernest Mathis.

It should also be noted that in 1996, Plymouth Whitemarsh High School (now Conshohocken's district) won a state championship in basketball under Head Coach Al Angelos and another state championship in 2010 under Head Coach Jim Donofrio.

Perhaps Conshohocken's greatest moment in basketball came back in 1904–5, with a team known as the Giants. They posted a 32-8 record, beating teams in four different states (a great distance to travel back then). With no other teams remaining to beat, Conshohocken was declared world champion of professional basketball. Years later, officials at the Naismith Memorial Basketball Hall of Fame, upon reviewing records, also declared Conshohocken to be professional basketball's first world champions. A photograph of the team is prominently displayed in the national Basketball Hall of Fame.

Members of the 1904–5 team included Steve White, Bill Keenan, Charles Bossert, Allan Glassey, Bill Herron, Billy Bennet and George Huzzard. Billy Neville was the team coach, and Johnny O'Keefe was the team mascot. The team led the league in scoring with 1,548 points on the season, an average of 38.7 points per game. In an era when final scores were typically 16–10 and 12–8, Conshohocken's 38.7 points per game was more than most teams could handle.

In 1927, the Conshohocken Church League was formed. It was discontinued for a few years during World War II and then resumed until 1964. Six churches participated in the decades-long league: St. Mark's Lutheran, Calvary Episcopal, St. Matthew's Catholic, United Presbyterian, First Baptist and Balligomingo Baptist of West Conshohocken. Names remembered from the Church League include Whitey Mellor, Chot Wood, George Snear, the Irwin brothers (Bob, Jack, Charlie and Ed), Harry "Tinker" Rowan, Art Freas, Bob Carroll, Lou Devaney, Ernie Pettine, Truman Drayer, Dave Johnstone, Gordon Atkins, Frank Milon, Ted O'Brien, Jim Kriebel, Ted Speaker, Dan O'Donnell, Knute Lawler, Sammy Webster, Jack Graham and Joe Bate, just to name a few.

Conshohocken today hosts what could be the oldest high school basketball tournament of its kind in the country. Every March for the past fifty years, the Fellowship House has hosted this tournament that has players participating from four different states. In 1961, the former executive director of the Fellowship House, Albert C. Donofrio, founded the tournament with four teams. In 2010, Executive Director Darlene Hildebrand reported a thirty-two-team tournament. Since the tournament's founding, more than two hundred players who have passed through the Fellowship House as part of the Albert C. Donofrio Tournament have been drafted into the National Basketball Association.

# And All the Rest

As we turn back the yellowed pages of the Conshohocken sports history, we find a lot to read about. Conshohocken's tug of war team grabbed a lot of headlines in the early part of last century, when it was Montgomery County champion from 1907 to 1910. John J. Fitzgerald managed the tug team,

For nearly sixty years, the Conshohocken Fellowship House has been a great outlet for the borough's children. Basketball is one of many activities provided at the youth center; other activities include computer rooms, weight room, a game room and dozens of group activities.

which was successful thanks in part to "Big Phil," who anchored the team. Other tug members included John "Ace" Reilly, James McDade and Joseph Kelly. Keep in mind that tug of war was a very popular sport back then, as it was an Olympic sport from 1900 to 1920.

The Conshohocken Bocce Club was formed in 1929 and brought many bocce championships to this fine borough over the years, not to mention many shuffleboard league titles. The Bocce Club located on West Third Avenue has revived the sport in recent years, making the outdoor courts a beehive of activity on hot summer nights.

Tennis became a major sport in Conshohocken in the early 1920s, when some of the greatest tennis players of the day would play before a gallery of hundreds of spectators at the Santa Maria Country Club. Bill Tilden played the club; at the time, Tilden was regarded as the greatest tennis player in the world. Vinnie Richards, Carl Fischer, Wallace Johnson, Bill Johnson and many other great players of the day would often use one of the three courts at the club. The Santa Maria Country Club is now part of the Spring Mill Fire Company.

The Conshohocken Tennis Club played on the five courts at the Conshohocken A Field throughout the 1920s, '30s and '40s, with players including George Rafferty, Alan Moore, Lloyd Montgomery, John Harrison and Betty Davis.

Conshohocken had two pigeon-flying teams—the Conshohocken East End Club and the Conshohocken Homing Club—in the Montgomery County division of a league that involved several states. Pigeons would often be shipped to other states for release with several other teams and fly a distance of one hundred miles. Charles Mosakowski of Conshohocken was a leader in the sport for many years throughout the 1930s and '40s.

The Conshohocken Soccer Team was all the rage back in the 1920s, according to the *Conshohocken Recorder*'s yellowed clippings. Hundreds of townsfolk would board trains on the weekends to view with pleasure the away games. Guys like Thompson, Wood, McGuire, Armour, Sutcliffe, Marland and Winterbottom would often stand out for the locals.

Conshohocken had a number of gun clubs dating back as early as the 1890s. The Washington Gun Club of 1898 would often host shoots with other clubs from Norristown, Radnor and Philadelphia. Many of these shoots would be held at the Ninth Avenue site. In the 1930s, Johnny Rigg, Charlie Todd, Vic Carnem, Bob Lampkin, Walter Beaver and E.J. Morgan were outstanding marksmen. Rigg, Todd and Beaver for many years played on the national stage, capturing national titles. In the early 1960s, Conshohocken was still represented by the Winters Junior Rifle Club, which would often travel to destinations like Harrisburg for competition. A few of the members of the 1960 team included Ronald Montemayor, Paul Borusiewicz, Billy Ciavarelli, Dave Zadroga, George Risell and John and Doug Holland.

Pool, anyone? That's right, and lots of it. In the 1920s and '30s, Conshohocken had more taverns and bars than Lee had tires, and most of those drinking establishments had pool tables, which led to the establishment of dozens of pool leagues throughout the borough. Statistics and league standings were printed in the brittle pages of the *Recorder* among the high school standings and results of the midget leagues. Lifelong Conshohocken resident Bob Pfanders is currently a nationally ranked pool player.

Professional wrestling staged at the Conshohocken Center Stadium drew large crowds for more than a decade in the 1950s with top-notch wrestlers like Antonio Rocca (the South America champion), Kid Fox and the Graham Brothers, along with the female wrestlers, father and son teams and all the big-name tag teams. Outdoor wrestling at the stadium became a great family event every summer, and crowds of more than one thousand spectators would enjoy the events.

The late Johnny Hannon carried the torch for Conshohocken when it came to dirt track racing. Hannon worked out of Galie's garage, once located in Connaughtown. Following a successful 1934 season, Johnny was invited to the 1935 Indianapolis 500. On his first qualifying round, Hannon skidded across the track, through a concrete retaining wall and was killed instantly. Hannon was inducted into the National Sprint Car Hall of Fame in 2006 at the seventeenth annual induction ceremonies.

Perhaps one of Conshohocken's greatest sports for more than forty years was boxing, going back to the 1890s. John A. Harrold, Conshohocken's first policeman and a pretty good boxer himself, set up a gym at his West Elm Street home and gave boxing lessons to borough children. Many of those students went on to be pretty good boxers, while several of them entered the pro ranks. Another Conshohocken resident who also set a gym up in his house in the early days was Tom Lanihan, who later conducted a boxing school. Some of Conshohocken's best-known professional fighters included Francis "Bunny" Blake, Jack Cavanaugh, John Kelly, Joey Blake, Anthony Rossi, "Midget Fox," Joey Hadfield, Johnny Craven, Wally Novak and Big John Casinelli.

Golf, "the rich man's sport" as it was once known, was very much a part of Conshohocken's landscape for many years. John Elwood Lee, who built his mansion at Eighth Avenue and Fayette Street in 1893, also built an eighteen-hole golf course behind his house. The course extended from West Sixth Avenue to Twelfth Avenue and from Forrest Street to Wood Street. In later years, the lower part of the course was used as a playing field for St. Matthew's football club. In the 1920s, Spencer Jones and Jack Davison represented the borough during golf tournaments, and throughout the 1940s and '50s, John Kelly was a very well-known golf pro.

When talking about bowling, the one and only name that rises to the top is Johnny Paul. Johnny was a well-known local professional who would travel to different parts of the country taking on some of the best bowlers. Throughout the 1950s and '60s, Paul would bowl in exhibitions with some of the top professionals in the business and beat them. Johnny sharpened his skills at Charlie Lutter's bowling lanes located in the basement of the Knights of Columbus Building at Second Avenue and Fayette Street. John Elwood Lee had his own bowling alleys above his carriage house, and for many years his team bowled in the Philadelphia Wholesale Drug League (try using that name today). Lee and his teammates, including Charles Herron, Sam Wright, Maurice Hallowell and James Wells, would travel the country to match up with other top-notch teams of the era.

Dave Traill excelled at two sports. He was a great pitcher in baseball, but he'll be remembered as one of two great swimmers of this borough, the other being Maddy Crippen. Crippen swam notionally for twelve years and won two national championships. She was also a member of the 1998 and 2003 world championship team and was Conshohocken's only Olympian, as she participated in the 2000 Summer Olympics and finished sixth in the four-hundred-meter individual medley.

Conshohocken has had a long love affair with soapbox derby racing, dating back to 1936, when Walt Cherry won the very first race on Spring Mill Avenue. Conshohocken also made its mark on the sport at the national level when Conshohocken champ Ed Myers traveled to Akron, Ohio, in 1974 to compete in the international Soap Box Derby Race. Myers set the record for the track's fastest time ever when he covered the 953-foot track in just over twenty-seven seconds, a record that still stands today.

Since the mid-1880s when Conshohocken began participating in sports, the town has offered up many of its citizens to the professional ranks and has provided the borough's residents with first-class teams and organizations. While there are many more events on the sports pages to discuss, it's time to turn the page to business—unless you want to talk about our top-notch marble tournaments back in the day, when Peter Gravinese and Adam DePietro ruled the marble world in Conshohocken.

Part Seven

# Business

## IT STARTED SLOW

Business in the borough limits grew as the town's population grew. In 1833, Conshohocken's business district consisted of one store and one tavern. These businesses mostly served the workers from the railroads and canal, as there were only six houses in the village back then. The six houses were all two- or three-room wooden structures with no indoor plumbing, and few even had outhouses. Outhouses in Conshohocken were commonplace into the 1940s. Keep in mind that Conshohocken didn't build a sewage treatment plant until 1937 at a cost of $219,000, and this led to one of the all-time great Conshohocken blunders.

In December 1937, borough engineers took on the great task of overseeing the installation of street laterals on each and every borough street. These would allow every resident to hook in to the sewer treatment plant for the use of indoor plumbing and bathrooms. And a fine job they did, with the exception of one omission: Borough Hall. That's right, when the town was plugged in to the sewer plant, borough officials found themselves with nowhere to go to the bathroom, as long as they were in Borough Hall, that is. Borough Hall was then located on the corner of Forrest and Hector Streets.

By the time incorporation rolled around in 1850, Conshohocken had started to develop a business district along Washington Street, what was then the main street in town. Activity centered on the canal, railroad and industry, with a few houses built along East and West Elm Streets. Before long, James Harry established a drugstore and brothers Sam and John Pugh

The old railroad station in Conshohocken, shown in its prime in 1890, has long been demolished, although a train station still stands on the site. This 1915 photo shows a Conshohocken newsstand in the Reading Station proudly displaying *Town & Country* magazines and the *Saturday Evening Post*.

established a coal and feed business. The Pughs later sold the business to Mr. Leroy and Mr. Williams.

By the mid-1870s, the borough's population exploded to more than 3,500 residents, and the business district started moving up the hill along Fayette Street. Businesses included James Wrigley's boot and shoe store on the corner of Fayette and Elm Streets. Aaron Beildeck's, located on Fayette Street below Elm, sold men's and boys' clothing. William Wright opened a hardware store at the corner of Hector and Fayette Streets, and Mrs. Stanley had a wonderful grocery store located on Hector Street below Cherry. Other retail business in the late 1870s included John Fair's Cigar's and Tobacco Shop, Joseph McGonagle's Furnishing and Undertaking Shop, J.D. Jones Groceries, Fulton's Dry Goods, James Tracy Flour and Feed Shop and Hallowell's Drug Store. James Holland owned the Grotto Oyster Saloon, and of course there were a few blacksmith shops on the edge of town, like the one owned by Joseph Chislett.

# Fayette Street Was a Boom

The absolute heyday of retail business in the borough came in the 1930s, '40s and '50s when, according to the 1930 census, Conshohocken had more than 230 retail outlets in the lower end of the borough and 17 registered hotels. Conshohocken was also at its highest population peak, with 10,815 registered residents in 1930 and 10,995 registered residents in 1950. In 1930, more than 250 residents were employed full time at retail businesses, not including part-time helpers.

A few of the Fayette Street businesses in the 1930s included Neville's Drug Store at First Avenue and Fayette Street, Kewson Grocery and Meats

Jack's Restaurant, owned by Jack Kornburger, once located on the corner of Second Avenue and Fayette Street, was a major hangout for borough teenagers who enjoyed the fountain sodas, milkshakes and hamburgers. *Standing, left to right:* Joe Touhey, Kay Walsh, Mary Burns and Paul "Roger" Touhey in 1950. Jack's later became the Spot and is currently Tony and Joe's Pizzeria.

J.A. Warrell's tire store, seen here at 23 Fayette Street during the 1940s, later expanded and moved into the former Knights of Columbus building at Second avenue and Fayette Street.

at 401 Fayette Street (long before Carl Aumann opened his diner) and Pater's Bakery at 38 Fayette Street. You could get a cheap haircut at Benny Guarino's barbershop. Let's not forget the White Bear Store at 527 Fayette Street, because it always gave out Green Stamps. Redmond's Shoe Store was a must stop at Easter time. Gabin's Hardware Store on the corner of Elm and Fayette Streets was always packed with customers, as was Jacobson's Men's Shop. Victor Frederick provided haircuts for twenty-five cents in 1935 from his barbershop at 822 Fayette Street.

You might just remember a few of these fine Fayette Street establishments, including Gold Seal Market, Shirley's Market, Conshohocken News Agency, Darby's Cigar Store, Nelson's Sweet Shop at 523 Fayette Street, Meaney's Radio and Auto Supplies, Murray's Cafe and Messenger's Hardware.

A few of the businesses along the avenues in the 1930s included Eberle Meats and Groceries at 400 East Tenth Avenue, Holden's Groceries and Oysters at Sixth Avenue and Wells Street, D'Alessandro's Liberty Food Store at Sixth and Maple Street, Altopiedi and Son Grocery Store at Fourth and Maple Street, Jerry Cardamone's Groceries at Ninth and Maple Street, Anthony Greco Groceries at Seventh Avenue and Maple Street, Pollock and Clark's Dairy at Seventh Avenue and Hallowell Street and Herbert Tole Meats and Groceries at Fourth and Harry Street.

If you needed a cold case of beer in 1936, John A. Kelly would sell you a case from his establishment at 918 Maple Street. A case of beer was $1.50, but if you wanted it delivered it cost $1.65. You could also buy your beer by the quart, gallon, eighth, quarter and half, and by the way, he sold fifty-eight varieties.

If you just wanted to stop for a quick one, Martinelli Cafe at Fourth and Wood Street had beer on draught. Stanley Chmielewski had his taproom conveniently located on the corner of Elm and Maple Street. Butcher's Place at 22 West Elm Street sold Schmidt's beer, and a little farther up Elm Street was the Connaughtown Inn. Sullivan Marine ran his fine establishment on Old Elm and Light Streets. The classy joint offered "Tables for Ladies." Victor Frederick ran the Bankers Bar at Second Avenue and Fayette Street for a couple of years; it later opened at Hector and Fayette Streets, with August A. Hoffman as proprietor and Eddie and Gus at the taps.

Just a few more fine Fayette Street establishments from the 1940s and '50s included Rafferty's Drug Store, Socket's Shoe Store, Cameo Beauty Shop, Jean's Beauty Shop, Wallace Jewelers, Rea Fashion Shop, Phillips and Son Gift Shop, Perfection Bakers and Carl's Sandwich Shop at Second Avenue and Fayette Street (later Jack's Sandwich Shop). And let's not forget Sam's Steak Sandwiches, McCoy's Pharmacy, Jack's Sea Food, the Highland Shop, Rea Fashion Shop, Conshohocken Bargain House, the Spot, Sam's Variety Store, J.A. Warrell's at Second and Fayette Street and one of the most popular Fayette Street stores of all time: Charlie Hicks Music Store, where one could buy all the latest Sinatra.

Just a few more for the memory file include Kehoe Brothers Hardware, the Frisco Beauty Salon at 401 Fayette Street, W.T Grants, Anthony's Barber Shop, Flocco and Sons Shoe Repair, Whitey Mellor's Sporting Goods, Adam Hager's Photo Studio, O'Donnell's Sporting Goods and Toys, the Highland Shop, Klein's Clothing, F.W. Woolworths, United Cigar Store, McGonigal's Drug Store, Zajac Shoe Store, Pat Lacey's Candy and Tobacco Store, Lekoe's Fashion Shop, A. Piermani and Son Beverage Distributors, the Sally Jane Shop, Mary Anna Shop, Nevin's Sunray Drug Store, Ray's Electrical Appliances, Flocco's Cancellation Shoe Store, Anthony's Men's Shop and Charles Hair Styling.

Enough of Fayette Street—but before we leave the business district, let's have a little fun and drink a few more suds. In the 1930s, the Community Bowling Academy opened at Second Avenue and Fayette Street, where dances were held. Rolling skating and bowling were also made available. Daniel Webster was the facility manager, and Charles Lutter was the proprietor. If the teens didn't go swimming at Pott's Quarry, they headed out to Marble Hall on the Ridge. Bubbling Springs at the tail end of Hector Street was a popular weekend hangout for many of the town's residents for decades. Art's Skateland on the Ridge was a great gathering place for many years, but for a really great night out, that meant going to the Riant Theatre on Fayette Street or the Forrest Theatre on Forrest Street. Of course, if you wanted to catch the train to Norristown, then the Grand Theatre, the Garrick Theatre or the Norris Theatre just might have the movie you wanted to see.

As teenagers, high school kids hung out at Jack's, the Spot or maybe enjoyed an old-fashioned milkshake at Neville's Drug Store. However, once they graduated from high school, drinks of a different kind were within eyesight, like going to Wally's Grill, Chippy's Maple Grill or Frank's Cafe at Seventh Avenue and Harry Street. The Village Tavern, located at 800 Spring Mill Avenue, was always a good hideout, as was the Spring Mill Hotel on Hector Street. Other drinking holes included DeMarco's Bar, Tommy Cowl's Fayette Grill, Montgomery House, Harrold's Hotel, later Zalik's Bar and Hotel, Pat Logan's Tavern or the Luna Café, where you could get beer or liquor, oysters or clams any style. Then there was Al's Bar on the corner of Elm and Poplar, Joe's Bar on West Elm Street, Carr's Tavern on upper Fayette Street, Ray's Tavern off Spring Mill Avenue, Paciello's Bar on lower Fayette Street and, of course, the granddaddy of them all, the Brown Derby. When one was finished drinking—not that anyone in Conshohocken ever drank too much—the Auch's buses ran up and down Fayette Street, or one could catch a ride with the Conshohocken Cab Company owned and operated by Reuben Stemple.

## FAMILY BUSINESSES STILL DOING BUSINESS

It started with names like Wood, Lee, Lukens and Jones. In later years, there were names like Leary, Harry, Krieble and Gravinese, and today businesses that carry on family names like Flocco, Civarelli, Del Buno, Lincul and Moore have all kept the Conshohocken business district grounded, with courtesy to the residents as the number-one business priority.

The Flocco family has been doing business and providing services in the borough of Conshohocken for more than eighty-five years. The family has owned and operated businesses on both sides of Fayette Street since 1926. Posing in this 1986 photograph, standing outside their store, members of the Flocco family include Joseph, Vincent Jr., Vince Sr., his brother Fred and Anthony.

Conshohocken's business district is much smaller than it was eighty years ago in 1930, but as in many small towns in America, these business owners know and understand their customer. It's about the courtesy extended, the grief shared with a loss, the overwhelming feeling that's shared when a customer announces a family newborn and the unlimited respect given to any stranger who chooses to do business with a family-owned business.

Businesses owned, operated and passed on to later generations of the families include the Flocco family's shoe and clothing business. The Totaros have been feeding familes for more than eighty years, and the Boccella family restaurants have been serving cheesesteak sandwiches for several generations. There are also family funeral directors the Moores, Snears and Ciavarellis, who have long buried members of the Conshohocken community, and Rudy Lincul, who has cut hair for nearly half a century, like his father Anthony who cut hair before him. Jimmy Del Buno continues to work seven days a week fixing, replacing and installing new roofs, like his father before him.

Family businesses new to the business district—Nick DiRenzo, a general contractor working with his son; DeStefano Electric; Coll's Custom Framing; the Great American Pub; Wilson's Gulf Station; Schank Printing; Spamps Restaurant; Ondik Insurance; and Storti CPA, just to name a few—are all passed along to the next generation from father to son or father to daughter.

Part Eight

# A Few Conshohocken Gems

## HANNIBAL HAMLIN, A GUEST OF THE WOODS

Whenever I say Hannibal Hamlin, the reply is immediate: "Hannibal who?" Hannibal Hamlin was the twenty-sixth governor of Maine and later the vice president of the United States of America. Hamlin served under President Abraham Lincoln during his first term as president from 1861 to 1865.

Alan Wood Jr., who built his home on East Fifth Avenue in 1859, became a United States congressman in 1866. While serving in Washington, D.C., he met and became good friends with Hannibal Hamlin, who would later spend time at the Woods' home in Conshohocken with Alan and his wife, Mary. Hamlin would occasionally spend the night as a guest of the Woods, marking the very first visit from a president or vice president, sitting or past, within the borough limits. The Woods' home was willed to the borough of Conshohocken in 1918 and is called the Mary Wood Park.

## GOVERNOR JOHN F. KENNEDY MISSES CONSHOHOCKEN

On a cold, rainy Saturday in October 1960, Senator John F. Kennedy was visiting the nearby Bala Cynwyd community. On the campaign trail for the presidency of the United States, Kennedy's motorcade was supposed to travel on Ridge Avenue in Roxborough, through Whitemarsh Township, on to Butler Pike and into Conshohocken. There was a ribbon-cutting ceremony scheduled at the borough line located at Thirteenth Avenue, with brief remarks from Kennedy and Conshohocken burgess James "Pat" Mellon. For

Hannibal Hamlin was the former vice president to Abraham Lincoln during Lincoln's first term as president of the United States from 1861 to 1865. Hamlin was a visitor to Conshohocken as a guest of Alan Wood Jr. and his wife, Mary. Wood, an East Fifth Avenue resident, became a United States congressman in 1866 and befriended Hamlin while serving his term in Washington, D.C.

unexplained reasons, the motorcade route was changed at the last minute, and Kennedy traveled the expressway and exited at West Conshohocken, missing Conshohocken. Senator Kennedy stopped at the War Memorial in West Conshohocken, spoke to the crowd in the rain for ten minutes and was on his way to Roosevelt Field in Norristown, with stops in Swedesburg and Bridgeport. As history now tells it, Senator John Kennedy was elected the thirty-fifth president of the United States just thirteen days after visiting West Conshohocken—thirteen days after missing his visit to Conshohocken.

Kennedy wasn't the only presidential candidate to miss Conshohocken. Theodore Roosevelt, making his third run for the White House, was scheduled to stop at the Reading Railroad station and deliver a three-minute speech to borough residents. On April 11, 1912, thousands of residents gathered at the station. Schools were closed so the students could gather to hear the former president speak; mills and factories along the river were shut down. Roosevelt's special train pulled into Conshohocken but never stopped. Roosevelt waved from the back of the train, but the train kept moving on to

Norristown. It was later explained that the conductor made a mistake and hadn't received word that Conshohocken was a stop.

## The First Lady, During and After

On September 20, 1994, First Lady Hillary Rodham Clinton visited Conshohocken to speak on the topic of healthcare. Mrs. Clinton headed a commission established by her husband, Bill Clinton, to come up with a healthcare reform legislation package. The first lady's conference was originally scheduled for a site in Bala Cynwyd but was changed to the Discovery School in Conshohocken at the last minute. Clinton's visit was brief, lasting about an hour and a half, but it marked the first visit by a first lady to the borough of Conshohocken.

Hillary Clinton returned to Conshohocken as a presidential candidate on Pennsylvania's primary Election Day, April 22, 2008. She spent two hours outside a polling place located at the Conshohocken Fellowship House. She was extremely gracious, speaking with everyone who came out in support of her. When the votes were counted later that evening, Clinton won the primary in the state of Pennsylvania, taking 55 percent of the vote over Barack Obama.

## Finally, Conshohocken Gets a Presidential Visit

More than 150 years after the borough's incorporation, Conshohocken finally got a visit from the president of the United States when George W. Bush came to the borough for the purpose of signing the Brownfield Revitalization Act into law. On Friday, January 11, 2002, more than one thousand residents stood in a steady rain to gain entrance into the Millennium Corporate Center, owned by Brian O'Neill, to hear the president speak. Mayor of Conshohocken Robert Frost called it a historic event, noting how proud he was at a time when the national spotlight was centered on the borough and its revitalization effort. The Bush motorcade crossed the Matsonford Bridge, to the delight of thousands of borough spectators, and following the event, the president spent time with many borough officials.

On January 11, 2002, George W. Bush, the forty-third president of the United States, pulled into Conshohocken as a guest of the O'Neill family and signed the Brownfield Revitalization Act into law. President Bush spent time with members of the O'Neill family following his speech to more than one thousand guests and residents.

# THE PINES

Few residents in Conshohocken today will remember "the Pines," once located at Ridge Avenue and Butler Pike. The property was originally a four-acre farm owned by the Yerks family, and in 1891, Mrs. Howard Wood, daughter-in-law of industrialist Alan Wood, rented the farm and prepared it for occupancy to give a holiday for girls who worked in the shops throughout Conshohocken. But Mrs. Wood found a greater need, using the property to give underprivileged mothers from the city of Philadelphia and their children a vacation for two weeks for each family in the summertime.

Mrs. Wood died in 1895, and her friends and family purchased the Yerks farm, rebuilt the barn to house up to 65 guests and set up a schedule to accommodate five two-week intervals, bringing as many as 375 mothers with their children each summer. The vacations for the mothers were paid for by charitable donations raised in Conshohocken by two groups, the Mothers of the Pines Club and Willing Workers.

# A Few Conshohocken Gems

The Pines, once located on Ridge Pike just off Butler, was formerly owned and operated by members of the Yerks family. But from 1892 to 1966, the old farmhouse served as a summer retreat for underprivileged mothers from the city of Philadelphia. The building was razed in 1967, and a six-story office building now occupies the site.

The twelve-day vacation for the mothers was spent relaxing and resting on lawn chairs placed under the spreading pine trees, while the children were kept busy with all-day events. Outdoor cooking and all cleaning were handled by a volunteer staff, and the evenings were filled with family events, singing and games.

The Pines operated for seventy-two years until 1966, when it was determined that the need for vacations in the country for working and underprivileged mothers and their children was less urgent than the needs of handicapped children. The Pines organization sold the property and donated more than $200,000 to the Child Development Center Pines Building, which was dedicated on October 13, 1966, and is still located at 1605 West Main Street in Norristown.

An engraved stone marker is located at the entrance of the Child Development Center Building and reads, "The Pines 1891, C.D.C. 1966," marking the date of the founding of the Pines and the date of the founding of the Child Development Center. The Pines buildings were demolished, and it is the current site of the Montgomery County SPCA and Whitemarsh Office Plaza.

## CONSHOHOCKEN'S ONLY HOSPITAL

World War I took a toll on the lives of Conshohockenites, and worldwide, sixteen million lives were sacrificed. The influenza epidemic that swept the world in 1918 killed an estimated fifty million people. One-fifth of the world's population was attacked by this deadly virus, forcing the borough of Conshohocken to open a hospital to handle the many flu-bitten residents.

The Conshohocken Calvary Episcopal Church, located at Fourth Avenue and Fayette Street, opened a forty-bed hospital, and within the first five days, four patients had died and thirty-three more patients were in comfortable hospital beds receiving the best of care. The Church Hospital was established in a matter of a few days. The managers of the Pines offered the entire fleet of iron bed stands, mattresses, bedding, linens and washstands.

Conshohocken schools and church services were canceled. No public gathering of any kind was permitted, and no residents were permitted to go to funerals if it wasn't a family member being buried. The second day the hospital was in operation, a young pregnant woman gave birth to a healthy baby girl. Within four days, family members removed the baby and took her directly to St. Mary's Church to be baptized.

Carroll Meyers was employed by the Schuylkill Iron Works and spent a few days touring the borough, checking in on the condition of employees. When he checked on an employee on Old Elm Street, he found the father and son very ill in bed, unable to care for themselves. The mother and daughter had died of the flu a week earlier. Both men were removed to the hospital, where they recovered. Had it not been for Meyers, they would have certainly died.

All residents traveling outdoors were asked to wear masks over their faces, and residents who had an ill family member were forced to hang a black scarf across their front door, warning potential visitors to stay away.

The influenza epidemic was gone as quickly as it started. When it was all over, seventy-eight Conshohocken residents lost their lives to the flu, ten West Conshohocken residents died and another forty-two residents passed away from the flu in Plymouth and Whitemarsh Townships.

The Conshohocken Calvary Church Hospital opened on October 12, 1918, and remained in service until October 29, 1918. Dozens of borough volunteers risked their lives to save hundreds of borough residents. Conshohocken had never had a hospital before the influenza outbreak, nor has it had one since.

When the schoolchildren were permitted to return to school later in the year, they would often play in the schoolyard, and the young girls would skip rope in rhyme with:

> *I had a little bird,*
> *Its name was Enza.*
> *I Opened the window,*
> *And in-flu-enza.*

## BISHOP MATTHEW SIMPSON, THE PRESIDENT AND CONSHOHOCKEN

Matthew Simpson was a Methodist bishop of Philadelphia who became very good friends with President Abraham Lincoln. The president would often summon Bishop Simpson to the White House for his opinion on important matters, stating that the bishop was more in touch with the common American and would understand the reaction to the situation, helping Lincoln to make decisions.

Bishop Matthew Simpson of Philadelphia visited Conshohocken in 1867 to help lay the cornerstone at the newly formed United Methodist Church being built on the corner of Elm and Fayette Streets. History tells us that Bishop Simpson was good friends with President Abraham Lincoln, and following Lincoln's assassination, Simpson gave what was called the "Great Eulogy" at Lincoln's graveside in Springfield, Illinois.

When President Lincoln was assassinated, his body traveled across parts of the country to his final resting place in Springfield, Illinois. On May 4, 1865, Bishop Matthew Simpson stood at Lincoln's graveside and gave what was described in history as the "Great Eulogy." And a great eulogy it was. The twenty-page document, found in the Abraham Lincoln Presidential Library, states in part, "Abraham Lincoln was a good man. He was known as an honest, temperate, forgiving man; a just man; a man of noble heart in every way." Thousands of mourners as far as the eye could see stood at the grave site, and not a dry eye was to be seen.

Stephen Miller of Conshohocken was an enlisted man in the Northern forces stationed in Washington, D.C., when Lincoln was assassinated. Miller was selected as a member of the Honor Guard in the president's funeral procession and was at the graveside when Bishop Simpson brought tears to the nation with his speech.

Just two years later, Stephen Miller and Bishop Simpson crossed paths once more when Bishop Simpson came to Conshohocken to lay the cornerstone and dedicate the founding of the Conshohocken United Methodist Church, built at the corner of Elm and Fayette Streets. Once again, Bishop Simpson gave a speech to the more than one hundred townsfolk in attendance before going back to Philadelphia.

## THAT'S RIGHT, OWNER OF THE PHILADELPHIA PHILLIES

William Baker owned the Philadelphia Phillies in the early part of the last century, and when he passed away in 1930, he left the team to his nephew, Gerald Nugent. Nugent was a Conshohocken resident for many years and lived on upper Fayette Street. Nugent ran into financial problems and was forced to sell the team back to the league in 1942. Nugent and his wife, Mae, and son Gerald Jr. lived in Conshohocken during his ownership of the Philadelphia team. Nugent's financial problems stemmed from the fact that he could never get more than three thousand fans into the ballpark at the Baker Bowl or Shibe Park.

Nugent owned the team during the midst of one of the longest streaks of futility in baseball history. From 1918 to 1947, the Phillies would have only one winning season—in 1932, when they posted a 78-76 record—and only finished higher than sixth place twice.

A little-known fact about one of Conshohocken's residents is that the one-time owner of the Philadelphia Phillies baseball club lived on Fayette Street. Gerald Nugent lived with his wife, Mae, and son, Gerald Jr., when he owned the Phillies from 1933 until 1942, when he was forced to sell the team back to the league due to financial problems. Nugent's teams never posted a winning record. Nugent is seen chatting with former Philadelphia As owner and manager Connie Mack.

## JUST A FEW MORE NAMES

"Chuck Wagon Pete," "Pete's Gang," "Uncle Pete." Francis X. Boyle was known to thousands of Philadelphia children for his television shows, where he made friends with the animals, drew many of his characters and displayed the most popular cartoons of the day. His shows ran from 1947, when he started with a show called *Chalk Talk*, until he passed away in 1967.

Peter Boyle lived on the 400 block of East Eleventh Avenue in Conshohocken for a number of years and would often lead the soapbox derby parade up Fayette Street on July Fourth. Peter's son, Peter Jr., went on to star in many movies and television roles, such as Frankenstein and the father on *Everybody Loves Raymond*. A little-known fact about Peter Jr. is that he was the best man in John Lennon and Yoko Ono's wedding in 1969.

International singing sensation Patty LaBelle was in Conshohocken to sing the National Anthem before the start of a football game at the Conshohocken A Field, located at Eleventh Avenue and Harry Street. Conshohocken mayor Robert Frost spent a little time with Patty following the ceremony and perhaps gave her a little advice on hitting the high notes.

John Street, the former mayor of Philadelphia, was born in Swedeland and grew up with his brother Milton on West First Avenue in Conshohocken. The Street boys attended Conshohocken High School and participated in many sports.

Jimmy Durante, "the Schnoz," was a regular visitor to Conshohocken for many years, as was Max Patkin, "the Clown Prince of Baseball." Patkin performed his baseball clown routine for minor league teams all over the country for more than fifty years.

We couldn't brag about Conshohocken without talking about music. One of the borough's well-known store owners was Charlie Hicks, an accordion player and orchestra leader. In the late 1930s, he was signed to a record deal after playing on a national radio show, and he played with his band all over the country.

In 2004, international singing sensation Patty LaBelle was in Conshohocken to sing the National Anthem before the start of a football game. The band Marah, whose founding members were born and raised in Conshohocken, have played all over the world with some of the biggest acts in music, including Bruce Springsteen. Founded by Dave Bielanko in 1993, the band has cut several major CDs. Dave's brother Serge later joined the band.

Eddie Cermanski, a West Conshohocken native and current Conshohocken resident, was one of the founding members of the Trammps. Cermanski was with the band in the 1970s and still plays occasionally with the band today. The Trammps became worldwide sensations in the disco era, when their music became part of the soundtrack in the movie *Saturday Night Fever*, starring John Travolta. Their hits include "Disco Inferno" and "Hold Back the Night," among others.

I wonder just how many residents remember Robert Ridarelli running around Conshohocken in the late 1950s and early '60s. Ridarelli, who later took the name Bobby Rydell, spent a lot of time playing on West Third Avenue, where his grandmother and aunts lived.

Has anyone seen Ernest Evans walking up and down Fayette Street? Well, Chubby Checker has been twisting his way in and out of his Fayette Street office for more than fifteen years. Chubby runs his food business out of the office in between his twisting appearances.

In 1971, the Conshohocken Town Council threatened to ban rock and roll forever from the borough of Conshohocken after Leon Russell rocked the Conshohocken A Field. More than thirty thousand rock fans from five different states showed up to see the "Jumpin Jack Flash" rocker perform. Fellowship House director Albert Donofrio staged the show, along with WIBG radio. Donofrio would never admit it, but it very well may have been his finest moment in Conshohocken.

Just as the Hooters hit the national music charts, they played a concert in the late 1980s at Archbishop Kennedy High School. Conshohocken has long been home to the Studio Four record company, located on lower Fayette Street. Acts have come and gone in the middle of the night to record in Conshohocken, like Billy Joel, Boyz II Men and Lauryn Hill. By the way, if you thought you saw Bob Dylan walking up and down Fayette Street a few years ago, you were right. He was in town to lay down a couple of tracks for the movie *North Country*, a 2005 drama for which Dylan featured four songs. Dylan spent time walking up and down Fayette Street and checking out our town.

Welcome to Conshohocken.

# About the Author

Jack Coll has been writing articles for dozens of publications for more than thirty years. His interest in Conshohocken and surrounding areas has led this award-winning photojournalist to establish a library of more than fifteen thousand photographs of the area. He has also authored several publications on locations in Montgomery County. Jack moved to Conshohocken in 1974 and has been married to his Conshohocken-born wife, Donna, for thirty-seven years. Jack and Donna's two children, Brian and Jackie, were both raised and still reside in the borough.

Jack has stayed involved in the community for more than thirty years as a member of the board of directors for the Conshohocken Fellowship House and a committee member for Mayor Robert Frost and the Mayor's Special Events Committee. He has played active roles over the years in the Conshohocken Soapbox Derby, the Conshohocken Car Show and dozens of other organizations, including the Conshohocken Merchants Association.

# About the Author

Jack is the owner of Coll's Custom Framing and Photography Shop, located on Fayette Street in Conshohocken, working with his son Brian. Brian has co-written a couple of books with his father.

For nearly twenty-five years, Jack has given slide show presentations on the history of Conshohocken to dozens of organizations in Montgomery County and has been a speaker at the local schools for both history and career days. In the past, Jack has taught students in the classrooms and given seminars on the art of photography.